The Curious World of Law

A compilation of legal (and some
non-legal) oddities

Dr John Kirkhope

PostScript Editions

Contents

1

INTRODUCTION

It is a pleasure for me to delve into the more dusty areas of our legal and constitutional traditions and for several years I have compiled slim booklets containing the results of my investigations, booklets that I have unashamedly forced upon friends and acquaintances but also sold to raise money for local charities. This volume is a collection of those booklets compressed into a single volume.

Readers will spot my love of heraldry from the following pages.

2

CURIOUS
COURTS

England and Wales have a complex system of courts many
of which most people would have never heard. For example, there is:

The Court of Swaincote

This is an ancient local court of verderers (effectively gov-
ernors) of the New Forest which has the power to try
minor crimes.

Barmote Courts

Which comprise, of course, a Great Barmote Court and a
Small Barmote Court. These are very old local courts in
Derbyshire which try matters relating to lead mining.

The Church of England

Has its own system of Ecclesiastical Courts which have jurisdiction to hear matters relating to church law. These courts have wonderful names, for example, the Chancery Court of York, the Arches Court of Canterbury and the Court of Faculties for whom I have acted as a Judge.

There are three Ecclesiastical Courts which are not over-burdened with litigants. These are:

The Benefices Act Court which was established under the Benefices Act 1898 for determining cases relating to benefices (grants of land made by the Church). *It has not sat since 1917.*

Court of Ecclesiastical Causes Reserved which is an appeal court having jurisdiction to hear cases relating to matters of ritual and doctrine. *It has sat only twice.*

Commissions of Review hears appeals from the Court of Ecclesiastical Causes Reserved. *Since the latter court has sat only twice it will be appreciated this court does not have great backlog of cases with which to contend.*

Court of Admiralty of the Cinque Ports

An ancient court, which has jurisdiction in Admiralty matters over the Cinque Ports. The Cinque Ports consist of 5 Head Ports, 2 Ancient Towns and 7 Corporate Limbs as follows: Faversham, Margate, Ramsgate, Sandwich, Deal, Dover, Folkestone, Hythe, Tenterden, New Romney, Lydd, Hastings, Rye and Winchelsea. They have a fascinating history. (Check their web site.) The Court last sat in 1914 and appeal is to the Privy Council.

Other courts which are noteworthy

High Court of Parliament

A feature of the United Kingdom's constitution, which it shares with other Commonwealth jurisdictions, is that the legislature, i.e. the Houses of Parliament, have judicial powers. A few of these remain, such as the power to try cases of impeachment, the quasi-judicial right to pass bills of attainder and the power to punish non-members of Parliament for contempt.

Impeachment is when a peer or commoner is accused of 'high crimes and misdemeanours, beyond the reach of law or which no other authority in the state will prosecute.' It is a procedure 'directed in particular against Ministers of the Crown.' It was last used in 1806 against Lord Dundas. In 2004 an attempt was made to impeach Tony Blair in matters concerned with the Iraq war.

A Bill of Attainder is an act of the legislature declaring a person or group of persons guilty of some crime and punishing them without the benefit of a judicial trial. Bills of Attainder were used, during the reign of Henry VIII, to execute Thomas Cromwell in 1540 and Catherine Howard in 1542. Henry VIII was the first monarch to delegate Royal Assent to avoid having to assent, personally, to the execution of his wife Catherine.

Any act or omission by a non-member which impedes either the Commons or the Lords in the performance of their functions may be treated as contempt. Parliament can summon a person to the 'bar of the House' to reprimand them, which last happened in 1957. They could order a fine which last occurred in 1666 which, in respect of the House of Commons, is a power regarded as lapsed.

The House of Lords could still impose a fine and the New Zealand Parliament used this power in 2006. Parliament has its own prison and incarceration, at least theoretically, could be ordered. The House of Commons may order imprisonment until the end of a parliamentary session while the House of Lords may order imprisonment for an indefinite period.

I was once threatened with being imprisoned in the Parliamentary prison, but that's a story for another day.

High Court of Chivalry (Earl Marshal's Court)

This is an ancient court which is now concerned with matters relating to coats of arms and other heraldic achievements. It had not sat for 200 years until 1955 when it was revived to adjudicate in a dispute between Manchester City Council and Manchester Playhouse. It may sit again if a similar dispute arises.

The Court of Claims

A court established before the coronation of each monarch for the purpose of hearing petitions from persons claiming the right to perform various functions at the coronation service. The Court was established in 1377 and last sat in 1952. It will be summoned again in 2023 when the coronation of King Charles is arranged.

There are a number of persons who have functions to perform at a coronation. These include the Lord Great Chamberlain, Lord High Chancellor, Lord High Constable, Earl Marshall, Lords High Stewards of England, Scotland and Ireland, Principal Garter King of Arms and the Queen's Champion. Deciding who is entitled to perform those roles, if there is a dispute, is the function of the Courts.

Lord Lyon Court

This is a Scottish Court which deals with matters of heraldry, entitlement to Clan Chieftainship and all related matters. Its head is Lord Lyon, King of Arms.

If you, or an ancestor, are or were domiciled in Scotland and you or your ancestors are 'virtuous and worthy persons' or you are 'descended from a person with (Scottish) arms and you bear the person's surname' you may apply for arms. It is a court much loved by Americans, New Zealanders and Australians who claim Scots ancestry.

Courts Leet (the original Health and Safety Officers)

These were, and are, historical manorial courts in England and Wales. They were courts of record which were concerned with oaths of peacekeeping, good practice in trade and to try by jury and punish crimes committed within their jurisdiction. They also developed means to ensure adherence to standards in such matters as sales of food and drink and agriculture.

Many Courts Leet were abolished by the Administration of Justice Act 1977 section 23. The powers of the surprising number which remain were curtailed. Amongst those which continue to meet are:

Ashburton Court Leet – England

A Portreeve has been appointed since 820. Also appointed is an Ale Taster and Bread Weigher.

(*Port*, in Anglo Saxon times, meant a market or walled town. A *Reeve* was a high ranking local official. It became, in course of time, common to appoint a *Reeve* for each *Shire*, as in Devon*shire*, Dorset*shire* and so on. Thus *Shire Reeve* eventually became *Sheriff*.)

Laugharne Corporation – Wales

Laugharne Corporation shares with the City of London the distinction of being one of the only two remaining medieval corporations within the United Kingdom. It was established in 1291 and is presided over by a Portreeve. It holds a court leet every six months and a court baron every two weeks. The court baron deals with civil suits within the corporation especially relating to land.

The Laugharne open field system is one of only two surviving and in use today in Britain. It is based on medieval strip farming.

Taunton Court Leet – England

This Court appoints *Rhine Ridders* who look after sewers and *Shamble Keepers* who oversee butchers, vegetable markets and ale tasters.

(*Shambles* from the medieval *Shamel* meaning bench or booth and *Flesshammel* meaning to do with flesh thus the street of butchers.)

Wareham Court Leet – England

The Court checks the quality of leather goods, weighs samples of local bread and tastes and reports on the quality of local ale.

Warwick Court Leet – England

Appoints an Ale Taster, Brook Looker, Pavement Looker, Surveyor of Buildings and a Herald who reports on the four court days.

3

OLDEST, LONGEST AND FIRST

Oldest continuously operating school in the world

The King's School, Canterbury was founded in 597 AD, over 1400 years ago. It is a selective public school (which means it is a private school).

Oldest Charity in the United Kingdom

The Hospital of St Cross and Alms House of Noble Poverty, which can still be found at St. Cross Road in Winchester, was established between 1136 and 1139. It continues to provide *'Wayfarer's Dole,'* which is a cup of ale and piece of bread, but only if you call at the Porters Lodge and ask for it.

The Oldest Judicial Appointment in the World

The Queen's Remembrancer is the oldest judicial post in the world having first been created in 1154. The function is to '... put the Lord Treasurer and Barons of Court in remembrance of such things as were to be called upon and dealt with for the Benefit of the Crown.'

Time Immemorial

Within England and Wales this means time extending beyond the reach of memory. In law it signifies that a property or benefit has been enjoyed for so long the owners don't
have to prove how long it has been in existence. Under the
Statute of Westminster 1275 it is fixed as beginning on 6
July 1189, the start of the reign of Richard I.

The Oldest Statute Law in the United Kingdom

The Distress Act 1267, also called the Statute of Marlborough, makes it illegal to seek 'distress' or compensation for
damage by any means other than a suit of law. In other

words it outlawed private feuds. Four of the original 29 chapters are still in force.

Cathedral Constables

Under a procedure which dates back to Edward I (1239-1307) Cathedral Deans are granted the authority to appoint constables to keep the peace in and around cathedral precincts. Five cathedrals in England continue to employ constables. They are Canterbury, York Minster, Liverpool, Chester and the yard beadles at Westminster Abbey. Under the Ecclesiastical Courts Jurisdiction Act 1860 they still have powers of arrest in respect of disruptive behaviour within a cathedral church.

The Oldest Branch of the Legal Profession (of which you have never heard)

The history of Notary Publics goes back to the Roman Empire. The first Notary recorded in England was a certain Swardius who drew up a grant of land in the eleventh century for Edward the Confessor. Thus Notaries pre-date Barristers and Solicitors by over 250 years. Originally appointed by the Pope, since 1279 they have been appointed by the Archbishop of Canterbury, to whom the Pontiff had delegated his power. Following the break with the Church of Rome, Notaries are now appointed under an

'Act Concerning Peter's Pence and Dispensations' (The Ecclesiastical Licensing Act 1533).

First Royal Flushing Toilet

Elizabeth I was the first monarch to have her own flushing loo known as 'Ajax.' It was designed for her by her godson Sir John Harrington in 1596, whom she had earlier banned from court for telling smutty stories.

The World's First State Lottery

Lotteries have been around since Roman times but it is thought the first State Lottery was held in England during the reign of Elizabeth I on 11 January 1569. There were 40,000 tickets each costing ten shillings. First prize was £5,000 (about £1.5 million in today's terms). A subsidiary prize was freedom from arrest for a week but not for serious crimes!

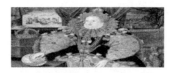

The Longest Legal Case in English Legal History

This case, entitled *The King v City of London,* concerned Smithfield Market in London. The lawsuit was started by James I in 1613. He claimed the Crown owned the market, a claim the market holders disputed. The case was adjourned in 1614. There was a Charter in 1638 and legal skirmishes in 1855 and 1860. The lawsuit was resuscitated in 1992. It was finally resolved in 1994 in favour of the City of London in the matter of *Crown Estate Commissioners v Corporation of City of London* (1994).

4

SURPRISING ROYAL APPOINTMENTS

There are several curious and joyous Royal Appointments some of which are set out as follows:

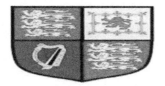

Grand Carver of England/Master Carver of Scotland

The great virtue of these appointments is that no one knows what the holders are intended to 'carve' or indeed what obligations they have. The present holders

are the Earl of Denbigh and Desmond and Sir Sebastian
Anstruther respectively.

Royal Limner of the Royal Household of Scotland.

The role dates back to 1581 and the present occupier of the
office is Elizabeth Blackadder. The function of the Royal
Limner of Scotland is to paint portraits of members of the
Royal Family and their residences.

Counting the Royal Chessmen

The Owner of Kingston Russell in Dorset has the task of
counting the Royal Chess pieces and storing them away
after a game. Not a very onerous task it has to be said.

Yeoman Bed Goer/Yeoman Bed Hanger

These appointments are still made although their role is redundant. It dates back to the time when the Royal Bed-chamber was examined before the Sovereign retired to ensure no miscreant was hiding in the arras!

Queen's or King's Champion

This role dates back to 1377 and has been in the Dymoke Family since that time. At one time, before a coronation, the Queen's or King's Champion would challenge anyone who doubted the right of the person about to be crowned. The present Champion is John Campion Fane Dymoke who is a chartered accountant. His father was a Lieutenant Colonel in the Army which you may regard as rather better training.

The Washer of the Sovereign's Hands

This role has been in the 'hands' of the Houison Crauford family since the 16th Century. They have a special bowl and towel and every year they write to the Sovereign and offer to wash her/his hands, an offer which the late Queen has always politely declined. Traditionally the hands of the Sovereign are washed just before the Coronation and thus the last time this happened was in 1953 when the late Queen was crowned. The Housin Craufords may well find their offer is accepted next time they make it, but by King Charles.

5

UNUSUAL RIGHTS OF THE SOVEREIGN

The Sovereign is Head of State and has many formal constitutional rights and obligations about which voluminous tomes have been written. The following is a list of the more obscure and idiosyncratic rights which the Sovereign enjoys.

Wardwick of the North Moor

There are 398 acres of land on the Somerset Levels the ownership of which comes with the title Wardwick of the North Moor, originally created by Alfred the Great in 878. The owner of the title has the obligation of escorting the monarch across the Levels should he or she need to escape in time of war.

The Owner of Sauchlemuir Castle

Must set out three glasses of port on New Year's Eve for the ghost of the grandmother of James IV of Scotland (1473-1513). It is not clear for which of his grandmothers, who were Dorothea of Brandenburg and Mary of Guelders, the port is required.

The owner of Fowlis

Must deliver, when requested, a snowball in mid-summer.

The City of Gloucester

Pays for its holdings of Crown Lands by providing to the Sovereign an enormous pie made of lampreys on Coronations and Jubilees. It's worth noting Henry I died of a surfeit of lampreys. The last time such a pie was presented was on the sixtieth jubilee of the late Queen's accession to the throne and to everyone's shame the lampreys had to be imported from Canada. Lampreys will be on the monarch's menu again in 2023 when King Charles's coronation takes place.

Great Yarmouth

Must provide, annually, a hundred herrings baked in 24 pasties to the Sheriff of Norfolk, who then sends them to the Lord of the Manor of East Carlton, who then sends them to the Sovereign. I cannot begin to imagine what the Sovereign does with the pasties when they arrive.

Hungerford has to present a red rose to the Sovereign in exchange for fishing and grazing rights.

The Duke of Marlborough

Has to present to the Sovereign a small satin flag bearing the *Fleur de Lys* symbol on 13 August, the anniversary of the Battle of Blenheim.

The Duke of Wellington

Has to present a French Tricolour to the Sovereign before noon on the anniversary of the Battle of Waterloo on 18 June.

The Duke of Atholl

Pays, by way of a rose, whenever the Sovereign calls. This was last done in the reign of Queen Victoria.

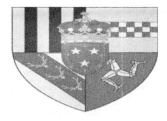

The tenant of Kidwelly Castle in Wales

Has to produce a bodyguard in full armour when the Sovereign passes nearby (though what constitutes *nearby* has never been established). Monty Python and the Holy Grail was filmed at the castle.

The Marquis of Ailesbury

The owner of Savernake Forest, has to produce a blast on a hunting horn should the Sovereign pass through the forest, which last happened in 1943.

The owner of Dunlambert Castle in Northern Ireland

Also has to produce a blast on an ancient bugle should the Sovereign pass by.

Bailiwick of Jersey

The Seigneur of the Bailiwick of the Parish of Trinity on the Island of Jersey must present two dead mallards if the sovereign visits. Sadly the last time the late Queen called on Jersey the mallards had to be imported from France.

Isle of Sark

The Seigneur of the Isle of Sark must pay £1.79 to the Sovereign each year. This dates back to the time of Elizabeth I. I have written a monograph on the constitutional position of Sark if anyone is interested.

British Virgin Isles

Must pay one bag of salt for the use of Salt Island to be presented on the Sovereign's birthday.

Royal Fish, being whales, dolphins, sturgeon and porpoise, under an Act of Parliament *De Prærogativa* 1324, belong to the Sovereign except for those washed up in Cornwall. It was always said the 'head belonged to the Queen while the tail belonged to the King' which is strange since whalebone, useful for corsets, is contained within the head while the tail contained blubber, meat and whale oil.

The Land in England and Wales is owned by the Sovereign. People will be familiar with the expressions 'freehold' and 'leasehold.' This means people have an 'interest' in land but do not own the land itself. Only the Sovereign is capable of owning land called *'allodial land.'* This dates back to the feudal system originating from the time of William the Conqueror.

Gold and Silver Mines (Royal Mines) are the property of the Sovereign and a license has to be obtained before these minerals can be mined.

Right to wrecks belongs to the Sovereign except wrecks which happen in Cornwall.

Right on Bona Vacantia, or the estates of those who die without legal heirs, reverts to the Crown except for those in Cornwall.

Right to the foreshore and riverbeds and territorial waters to the Continental Shelf, except for those foreshores privately owned and the foreshores in Cornwall, are the property of the Crown.

The Royal Navy

The Sovereign in theory owns the Royal Navy and retains
the right to press men into the service.

Seigneur of Swans

The Sovereign, one of whose titles is Seigneur of Swans,
owns all unmarked mute swans, except for those in Orkney
and Shetland, and is the only person entitled to eat one.
They probably taste like chicken!

Driving Licence & Passport: The Sovereign has no need of
and does not have either document.

There are many other rights of the sort set out above but, frankly despite evidence to the contrary, I have better things to do with my life then set them out.

6

EXPLODING
SOME MYTHS

Introduction

Some while ago I volunteered myself to give talks on cruise ships. Having put myself forward I then had to find topics on which to talk. By far the most successful was the lecture which has enjoyed various titles, but most recently 'Peculiar Laws, Ancient Customs and Curious Courts'. As I always start by explaining to my audience, rather pompously I will admit, it is a 'melange' or a wander through the musty corridors of our legal system. I am a geek, the legal equivalent of the train spotter. Obviously I don't, anymore, wear an anorak or hang around on station platforms. In other words it is a collection of legal 'odds and ends' which I find interesting and/or amusing.

I must explain some technical issues. In what follows I am concerned, largely, with the laws of England and Wales. The legal system within those countries does not recognise the principle of *desuetude* (which means, broadly, that a law may fall into disuse). In other words if a law, no matter how old, remains on the Statute Book it remains good law. Expressed another way what follows are descriptions of current law and *not* an exercise in examining and laughing at the ancient or former laws of our ancestors.

Finally this is a work in progress. It is constantly being updated as I stumble across another curiosity of the English legal system.

If you Google something like 'Strange Laws' or 'Unusual Laws' you will get a variety of answers, most of which are not true. My current favourite is: 'There is a law in Ohio which makes it illegal to get fish drunk.' Completely untrue.

Similarly you often find various myths repeated, with regard to English Law, because no one has bothered to check. These are a few of the more unusual or amusing examples I have found.

It is illegal to die in Parliament.

False. This seems to arise from the idea that if you die in Parliament you are entitled to a state funeral. At least four people have met their end in Parliament. These were *Guy Fawkes* and *Sir Walter Raleigh* who were executed in 1606 and 1618 respectively in the Old Palace Yard – for obvious reasons no one suggested they had a state funeral; *Spencer Perceval* who was assassinated in 1812, the only United Kingdom Prime Minister to meet his end in this way; and *Sir Alfred Billson* who died in 1907 while casting his vote in Parliament. Neither Spencer nor Sir Alfred received a state funeral.

It is illegal to place a stamp of the Sovereign upside down on a letter.

False. This seems to arise from a misreading of The Treason Felony Act 1848.

It is illegal not to carry out at least two hours of longbow practice a week.

False. This was true under the Unlawful Games Act 1541. However, that Act was repealed by the Betting and Gaming Act 1960.

It is illegal for a commoner to permit his animal to have carnal knowledge of a pet of the royal household.

False. There is no evidence any such law ever existed.

It is legal to shoot a Welshman with a longbow on Sunday in the Cathedral Close in Hereford; or inside the city walls of Chester after midnight; or to shoot a Scotsman within the city walls of York, other than on Sunday.

False. Killing people is generally regarded as a bad thing and something to be discouraged and is, therefore, unlawful regardless of who they are or when or where you kill them!

It is legal for a pregnant woman to relieve herself anywhere she likes including a policeman's helmet.

It is legal for a man to urinate in public as long as it is against the rear offside wheel of his motor vehicle and his right hand is on the vehicle.

Both are false. Commonly thought both equally distasteful and untrue.

Finders Keepers – Losers Weepers.

False. There persists the idea that if something is found which has been lost the finder becomes the owner. This is false. It is a crime called 'Theft by Finding.' There is an obligation to make reasonable efforts to trace the owner. If the finder is unsuccessful then the situation may change.

7

PARTICULAR LAWS

I would ask my readers to bear in mind I am concerned with current laws.

It is illegal to enter the Houses of Parliament wearing a suit of armour.

True, under the Statute Forbidding Bearing of Armour 1313.

You cannot gamble in a library.

True, under the Library Offences Act 1898.

You cannot 'operate a cow' when you are intoxicated or while in possession of a loaded firearm.

True, under the Licensing Act 1872. In fact under the same Act it is illegal to be intoxicated while in possession of a loaded firearm or to be drunk in charge of a carriage, horse or steam engine.

It is illegal to be drunk in a pub.

True. Under the Licensing Act 1872 section 12 'every person found drunk ... on any licensed premises shall be liable to a penalty.' See also the Metropolitan Police Act 1839 and the Licensing Act 2003.

It is illegal to handle a salmon in suspicious circumstances.

True. This is an offence under the Salmon Act 1986. *For the avoidance of doubt I will not enter into correspondence about what constitutes 'suspicious circumstances.'*

You must give notice if you intend to import potatoes from Poland.

True. This follows from the Polish Potatoes (Notification) (England) Order 2004. I have no idea why.

It is illegal to cause a nuclear explosion.

True. This was made an offence under the Nuclear Explosions (Prohibitions and Inspections) Act 1998. You might have thought this is obvious and hardly needed an Act of Parliament. Oddly the Act extends to the Sovereign and the Prince of Wales but if either one does cause a nuclear explosion they are exempted from criminal sanction. *Well that's OK then!*

A London Cabby may not carry rabid dogs or corpses and they must ask passengers if they have smallpox, cholera, relapsing fever, typhus and the plague. If they do carry pas-

sengers sadly infected then they must disinfect the cab and advise the authorities.

True. This follows from the Public Health (Control of Diseases) Act 1985. *So next time you hail a London cab remind him to ask you the appropriate questions and wait and see what response you get!*

Those living in Devon and Cornwall have the right to re-move sand from beaches for agricultural purposes.

True. This right dates from a Charter granted by Richard, Earl of Cornwall in 1235. It is now included in an Act of Parliament entitled Sea-Sand (Devon and Cornwall) Act 1609.

The Case of Richard Pendrell.

Richard Pendrell helped Charles II escape after the King had been defeated by Cromwell's forces at the Battle of Worcester in 1651. Charles II resumed the throne in 1660 and in 1662, as evidence of his gratitude, he granted Richard Pendrell and his descendants an annuity of £100. The annuity, as far as I am aware, is still being paid.

8

THINGS YOU
MAY NOT DO
ON A PAVEMENT

The following are not permissible under the Highways Act 1835 section 72, Metropolitan Police Act 1839 (sections 54 and 60) and/or the Town Police Clauses Act 1847 section 28.

It is illegal to:

Carry a plank *(sadly I have tried researching to see if there is a legal definition of a plank without success)*;

To carry a ladder or pole;

Play annoying games;

Slide on snow and ice;

Slaughter cattle;

Keep a pigsty *(unless it is hidden)*;

Order a servant or permit a servant to stand on a sill of any window above a pavement for the purposes of decoration or repair. *(This provision has caused me great inconvenience. Many a time I have ordered my servants onto the window sills to carry out necessary repairs or decorations and they have refused!)*;

Ride a horse or bicycle or motor vehicle upon a footpath set aside for foot passengers. *(Following the case Taylor v Goodwin 1879 a bicycle is a carriage for this purpose. Just try telling someone riding a bike on a pavement they are a carriage and should be on the carriageway. The response is likely to be challenging.)*

Shake or beat any carpet or rug in any street. However, it is allowed before 8 a.m. *(Quite right – carpet beating after 8 a.m. is obviously wrong!)*

9

YOUR HOME IS YOUR CASTLE?

There are, by some calculations, 20,000 Local Authority Officials who have the right of entry into your home. That is to say without a warrant or a police presence. Some examples of the provisions under which they demand entry are as follows:

Under the Plant Health Order (2005) to investigate whether pot plants have a pest or plant passport;

Hypnotism Act 1952 to ensure no illegal or unregulated hypnotism is taking place;

Anti-Social Behaviour Act 2003 to ensure hedges are not too high.

It is suggested that there are some 1000 powers allowing Local Authority Officials to enter your home!

10

AND IT'S NOT JUST US!

Thailand   It is illegal to step on money because coins and notes display the King's head and the King is revered in Thailand;

Spain   It is illegal for butcher to sell a rabbit without its head to ensure they do not try to sell cats instead of rabbits;

France   In the parish of Sarpourenx it is illegal to die unless you have previously purchased a plot in the cemetery;

USA   Although this may change, the USA has for decades prohibited the import of haggis because it contains offal. Americans are clearly not aware of the contents of the average burger;

Switzerland   You may not flush a toilet after 10 p.m. Clearly Swiss men do not have the same problems with their prostates as men in the UK;

Hong Kong   A wife may kill a cheating husband as long as she does it with her bare hands;

Iowa, USA   People who are blind may apply for and be granted a licence to own a gun.

11

THOUGHTS AND COMMENTS REGARDING LAWYERS

Introduction

As I explained in the introduction to this volume, for several years I have annually produced slim booklets containing a miscellany of curious or interesting facts. Frankly I have done it less for the amusement it gives others, I hope, than for the fact it represents, for me, a form of relaxation. It started as a gift for my family, as an alternative to Christmas cards. I am pleased that it does appear to give pleasure to a wider audience and copies have been sold and raised money for Weston super Mare Museum, Weston super Mare General Hospital and my parish church Corpus Christi. I have even been asked when the next issue will be produced which is gratifying. If it makes people smile then I have succeeded.

Much of what follows in this section was produced to celebrate the twentieth wedding anniversary of my wife, Lisa, and myself, (who would have thought it), and my seventieth birthday.

As before the matters included are an entirely arbitrary choice. The only thing they have in common is that I find them interesting and/or amusing.

Executed for overcharging

During the time of the Roman Empire the fees that could be charged by lawyers, called *tabellio,* were prescribed. The penalty for overcharging was death. (*Happy days I hear you cry!*)

Anon

'If it wasn't for lawyers we wouldn't need them.'

Winston Churchill

'Lawyers occasionally stumble over the truth but most of them pick themselves up and hurry off as if nothing had happened.'

George Bernard Shaw

'The average lawyer is a nincompoop who contradicts your perfectly sound impressions on notorious points of law; involves you in litigation when your case is hopeless, compromises when your success is certain and cannot even make your will without securing the utter defeat of your intentions if anyone takes the trouble to dispute them.'

What can you call a lawyer?

In the case of *Smith v Wood* (1693) it was decided you can call a lawyer a *rogue* and a *rascal*. However, you could not say, in those days, he was a *whoremaster* or as we would now say a *brothel keeper*. So now you know.

Getting In The Mood – Everyone Loves A Lawyer?

As a lawyer I have discovered you can never fail to get a smile if you tell an anti-lawyer joke. So to get everyone in the mood:

'Do you think we should send for a lawyer?'

'Certainly not. We're in enough trouble already.'

and

'You have an excellent case Mr. Peabody. How much justice can you afford?'

Also, and this is my favourite;

'What is your basic fee?'

'£100 to answer three questions.'

'Whoa. Isn't that expensive?'

'Yes. Now what is your third question?'

Finally

A lawyer is never entirely comfortable with a friendly divorce any more than a good funeral director wants to finish his job and then have the patient sit up on the table.

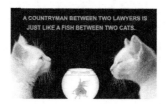

This is not an anti-lawyer joke but I came across this in a recent translation of the New Testament (The New Testament for Everyone Translated by Tom Wright (SPCK 2011) Mark 13 (38)

Jesus said: 'Beware of lawyers. They like to walk around in long robes and be greeted in the market. They take the best places at dinner parties. They devour the property of widows and make long prayers without meaning them ...'

I feel suitably chastened!!

12

ASK A STUPID QUESTION?

I have not been able to conduct rigorous research and, thus, cannot state with certainty the following courtroom exchanges are accurate. I can only say I do hope they are.

Q: And you all had a very intimate relationship didn't you Mrs. A?

A: *We had sex two times. It wasn't very intimate.*

Q: What is your date of birth?

A: *July 18.*

Q: What year?

A: *Every year.*

Q: Can you describe the individual?

A: *He was about medium height and had a beard.*

Q: Was this a male or female?

A: *Unless the circus was in town I'm going male.*

Q: Doctor how many autopsies have you performed upon dead people?

A: *All of them. The live ones put up too much of a fight.*

Q: Do you know how far pregnant you are?

A: *I will be three months on 8 November.*

Q: The date of conception was 8 August 8?

A: *Yes.*

Q: What were you and your husband doing at the time?

Q: Are you sexually active?

A: *Oh no. I just lie there.*

Q: The youngest, the 20 year old, how old is he?

A: *He's 20, much like your IQ.*

Q: Are you married?

A: *Yes.*

Q: What does your husband do?

A: *Whatever he's told.*

Q: How was your first marriage terminated?

A: *By death.*

Q: And by whose death was it terminated?

A: *Take a guess.*

Ken Dodd

In 1989 Ken Dodd, a much-loved United Kingdom co-
median, was charged with tax evasion. It was revealed he
had made numerous 'cash and carry' flights to Jersey and
the Isle of Man to deposit his earnings in up to twenty
different bank accounts. Surprisingly, in what on the face
of it was a cut and dried case, he was found not guilty
possibly because, it is thought, he entertained the jury. For
example, when asked by the Judge what it was like to carry
suitcases full of cash he replied:

'The notes are very light, M'Lord.'

When the prosecuting barrister confronted Mr. Dodd
with a damning affidavit from an accountant Dodd responded:

'But Sir the man is dead.'

The prosecutor replied:

'What matters is the evidence. Whether he is alive or dead is entirely irrelevant.'

Said Dodd:

'It's very relevant to him, Sir.'

13

CRUEL AND UNUSUAL PUNISHMENTS

1989 – Thailand

Chamoy Thipyaso was sentenced to 141,078 years for fraud (but will actually serve only 20 years).

2011 – Andalucía – Spain

A 25-year-old man took his parents to court after they stopped his pocket money of £355 per month. The judge ruled he had to leave his parents' house within 30 days and learn to stand on his own two feet.

2013 – Louisiana – USA

Albert Woodfox served 43 years in solitary confinement, spending 23 hours a day in a six-foot by nine-foot cell with an hour's exercise a day in a concrete yard, shackled and alone. This is the longest period of solitary confinement in USA prison history. He was released in 2013 after the Court of Appeal overturned his conviction.

2018 – Missouri – USA

David Berry was convicted of illegally killing hundreds of deer. He was sentenced to prison and ordered to watch Disney's 'Bambi' once a month.

2018 – Iowa – USA

In the 1990's Benjamin Schreiber was sentenced to life in prison without the possibility of parole after committing a murder. In 2015 he was rushed to hospital after a severe complication following gall stones. He technically died and was revived five times. He was returned to prison.

Schreiber claimed because he had died he had served his life sentence and should be released. The Iowa Court of Appeal was not convinced. They stated either the prisoner was alive and must remain in prison or was dead in which case the appeal was mute.

2019 – Wenzhou – China

Police in Wenzhou China are fining people who text while crossing the road on the basis they often put themselves and others at risk. The fine is small – about £1 – but since the ban was introduced in January 1000 people have been fined or warned.

I must say this is something I would support if introduced in the UK.

14

INCOMPETENT AND ANNOYING CRIMINALS

By far my favourite section!

Every year produces still more cases. Sometimes I would want to say to the criminals: *'If you devoted as much time and energy to pursuing an alternative "legal" career you could be very rich. Frankly as a criminal you are a failure: this was not a good career choice.'*

1970 – Japan

I am not sure this fulfils my criteria (but then I am not sure what my criteria are) but a drunken Japanese driver continued his journey for more than a mile before he noticed his left arm had been torn off when he'd collided with an oncoming lorry. A passing pedestrian found the arm and handed it over to the police while the driver reported the loss of the arm. Fortunately the arm was reunited, but not necessarily reconnected, with the owner.

1980 – Liverpool – England

Philip Aston was seriously injured when the car in which he a passenger collided with a traffic island. His civil action failed. The driver was his getaway driver, and Aston, along with other drunk men, had been fleeing the scene of a burglary they had just committed when the accident happened.

1981 – St Albans – England

A man was convicted of stealing a microwave oven and was given a suspended sentence and discharged. It was revealed during the trial that he thought he was stealing a television set. The Judge concluded it was unfair for someone so stupid to go to prison.

2008 – Ohio – USA

A Mr. Brewster and friend decided to attempt to rob a Domino's Pizza. In their rush to escape they ended up in the deep freeze in which, surprisingly, they were left to cool their enthusiasm for some little while.

2010 – Florida – USA

Raymond Stanley Roberts was arrested for drug possession. He said the first bag released from his anus containing cannabis was his, while the second bag containing cocaine was not his and he had no idea how it got there.

2011 – Meshchovsk – Russia

Victor Jasinski entered the hairdressing salon of Olga Zajac and demanded money from the till. Ms Zajac, alleged to be a karate black belt, floored him with kick, beat him senseless, tied him up, stripped him naked, attached him to a radiator, fed him nothing but Viagra pills and used him as a sex-slave for three days.

When questioned, Ms. Zajac stated: 'Yes, we had sex a couple of times, I bought him new jeans, gave him food and even gave him 1,000 roubles when he left.'

Mr Jasinski was given emergency treatment in hospital for badly swollen testicles.

2013 – Oregon – USA

Derrick Mosley decided he would rob a shop. He armed himself with a knife and a baseball bat. The problem was the shop he chose to rob was a gun shop. The owner of the premises drew his handgun and ordered Derrick to drop his knife and bat. When the police arrived they found the offender on the ground guarded by the shop owner.

2015 – Cavan – Ireland

Three men tried robbing a shop in Cavan in Ireland. The Gardaí arrived and they were arrested but not before one of them had run back into the shop to try and hide. In doing so he caught and tore his scrotum on a shelf. The criminal, while in prison, then tried suing the shop owner for the injury he had suffered. He failed.

2015 – Hollywood – USA

Lupita Nyong'o wore a dress to the Oscars which was said to be worth $150,000 and had, it was claimed, 6,000 real pearls sewn on. Thieves stole the dress and removed two pearls. They had them assessed and discovered they were not real. The robbers, in disgust, then returned the dress to the hotel leaving it inside a rubbish bag in a bathroom.

2016 – Manchester – England

Simon Crawshaw noticed a bathroom window had been left open. He climbed up a down pipe to gain access to the property via the open window, which was on the first floor of the building and promptly got stuck. He was left 'hanging out' for a while waiting for the police to arrive. He was sentenced to two and half years in prison.

2017 – Birmingham – England

A man noticed that an extractor unit had been removed and took this as an invitation to rob a fried chicken shop in Birmingham. He embarked on his enterprise at 2 a.m. The problem was he got stuck and remained stuck for the next seven hours at which point the Fire Brigade rescued him and the police arrested him.

2018 – Christchurch – England

Jamie Costello had indulged in drink and drugs, not wisely but well, to the extent he was 16 times over the drink/drug-driving limit. He endeavoured to out-run the police by attempting to make his escape on a lawn mower. Not surprisingly he was caught, charged and subsequently fined £200 and disqualified from driving for one year.

2018 – Merseyside – England

Mr. Terence Cole, who was 61, decided, when quite young, on a career robbing banks presumably on the basis that they are where the money is. His problem is that he was and is incompetent. To date he has accumulated 41 years in prison. After being released from his last sentence he was determined he would resume his chosen vocation.

He attempted to rob six banks and two betting shops. He covered his face so his victims did not clearly hear what he was saying. He mumbled: *'I have a gun.'* He was told to *'Sod Off'* during the course of one attempted robbery.

In only one theft was he successful but even then was unaware of the fact until he got to the railway station. Judge Goldstone Q. C., in sentencing Mr. Cole for eight years, stated*: 'Fortunately you are not very good at this.'* Something of an understatement you may think.

2019 – Wisconsin – USA

William Gallagher, who was 68, had recently been released from a 20-year jail sentence and returned to New Jersey after spending the majority of his adult life in prison. He was, he acknowledged, institutionalized. Every day he would look at his watch and imagine what he would be doing if back in prison. After doing some research he concluded the prison food in Wisconsin was the best to be had. Thus he travelled to that State to rob a bank. He demanded $100 and said he had a bomb. He also gave the bank cashier his name and told them to phone the police. During his trial he demanded he be sentenced to ten years in jail and was very angry when Judge Hansher, who was concerned about creating a new sort of tourist industry, refused to sentence him and asked for pre-trial reports. Mr. Gallagher is reported as saying: *'I thought we had a deal.'*

2019 – Denmark

I have always regarded the Danes as honest people but apparently there is an 'epidemic' of insurance fraud in Denmark. The Danes are making some £500 million per year claiming for fake accidents and self-mutilation.

A 55-year-old farmer, now retired, cut off his hand with an angle grinder and claimed it as an accident. The hand was reattached but had to be removed later. In 2011 he claimed he had been hit by a train which, he asserted, he had not heard because he was listening to music on his headphones. The courts decided it was no accident but a deliberate act. Thus not only did he not succeed in his attempted fraud but he is now minus one hand and one leg!

2019 – Bangor, Maine – USA

Having just robbed a bank Jason Mackenrodt made his escape by dashing across four lanes of traffic and a restaurant car park. However, he slipped on ice, dropped his gun and the money he had stolen blew away. The problem was, from Jason's point of view, his accident occurred in front of an off-duty policeman, Officer Glenn Lang, who immediately arrested Jason. Just a bad day at the office I guess.

2019 – North Carolina – USA

Burglars broke into a house and found an 11-year-old child who they locked in a wardrobe. They started to ransack the place. In the meantime the child escaped, grabbed a machete and attacked one of the burglars who kicked the child in the stomach. The child then attacked him again and was rewarded with another kick. By this time the criminal realised he was bleeding and fled. However the blood evidence left at the scene enabled the police to make an arrest.

2019 – Gympie – Queensland – Australia

A convicted murderer burnt off his ankle tag. The authorities became suspicious when the tag had remained in the same location for several days. Twelve days later they found the man, who had a gaping wound in his leg and severe bone infection. He was sent to hospital for treatment but it was too late to save his leg. The magistrate informed him he was paying the price for his stupidity.

2019 – West Monroe – Louisiana – United States

Ashley Beth Rolland was accused by her boyfriend of stealing $5,000 from him. He claimed she had stolen the money while he took a shower. Ms. Rolland admitted the theft and consented to an 'intimate' body search. The police officer found a wad of cash and a bag of drugs. Ashley denied ownership of the drugs and claimed she did know how they came to be concealed in her body.

2019 – Hampshire – England

Three criminals, Messrs. Joshua Pearce, Benjamin Pearce and Michael Antram, who have over a hundred past offences between them, stole mountain bikes from a garage. After throwing glasses and bicycle wheels at the pursuing police they ran into the sea. The police, after waiting for them to emerge from the ocean, arrested them. They were sentenced to between two and three years in prison.

2019 – Kent – England

Jan Gina broke into a house via the cat flap while the owners were asleep. He stole wine, clothes, a handbag etc. But clearly his endeavours caused him to feel peckish and before leaving he munched on a leftover fish cake. His downfall was the DNA he left on the half-eaten fishcake. The stolen property was recovered together with five bags of cannabis. Mr. Gina denied the burglary, saying he did not like fish. He eventually pleaded guilty and was sentenced to two years in prison.

2019 – Massachusetts – USA

On 15 May 2019 (my birthday!) Neil Roman returned home to realize someone had broken into his house. He smelled cleaning solvents and bleach. On closer inspection he discovered nothing had been stolen but, for example, his son's room, which had been messy, was now immaculate. Every room had been cleaned except for the kitchen. The toilet paper had been adorned with *'a neatly folded rose.'*

2019 – Minnesota – USA

Hilary Smith arrived home to find a thank you note on her porch which read as follows: *'So just a quick little thank you for leaving me the opportunity of stealing your package. Very nice of you.'* A package of goods she had ordered online had been left by the courier and then stolen.

2019 – Portugal

Individuals drilled a hole in a warehouse in Aveiro and stole many boxes of cod which, it seems, are very valuable.

2019 – Chorley – Lancashire – England

I am not sure whether this qualifies under the heading 'Incompetent Criminals' but I include it because I so enjoyed the headline, which appeared in the Lancashire Post on 3 September 2019, which was: 'Dancing Chorley flasher balanced pie on his head.' Steven Gaskell had, evidently, drunk not wisely but well. He appeared outside the Elephant and Castle pub in Chorley. He paced up and down, did a little dance, and then placed a pie on his head before 'exposing' himself. He has been found guilty of an offence. History does not record what flavour of pie Steven preferred.

23 December 2019 – Colorado – USA

David Wayne Oliver, after threatening the staff of the Academy Bank with the use of a weapon, robbed the said bank. He left the premises and started throwing the money all over the place while shouting: *'Merry Christmas.'* David then sat down and awaited to be arrested. Not all the money has been recovered!

2020 – Florida – USA

The police are looking for a man who broke into a house in Bradenton and sucked on a man's toes while he slept. The suspect declared to his 20-year-old victim he was there to 'suck toes.' Well that's OK then!

2020 – Kentucky – USA

Justin Carter was not so much incompetent as unlucky. He decided to rob a fried chicken bar which gloried under the name of 'Raising Cane's Chicken Fingers.' The bar was empty apart from a couple enjoying a night out. The problem, from Justin's point of view, was that the couple were Detective Chase McKeown and his wife Officer Nicole McKeown. When they saw what was going on they drew their guns and told the would-be robber to drop his weapon which he did. He then attempted to escape but was chased and apprehended. Another bad day at the office perchance!

2020 – Bournemouth – England

If you are engaged in a criminal enterprise you would have thought at least one consideration would be how to make your escape with the loot. Scott Hunt, who it would appear suffers from a number of afflictions including a gambling addiction, had lost £300 on various gambling machines on the day of the attempted theft.

He is also schizophrenic and tried stealing from a car in the early hours of the morning. However, he was rumbled by the car owner who used his remote key to trap him. The owner then phoned the police while Mr. Hunt was forced to sit in the car and wait to be arrested.

2020 – Monmouth – Wales

Jake Fletcher had successfully burgled two properties in Monmouth. In the third house he was confronted by Charlie, an orange winged Amazon parrot, who squawked and squawked and awoke its owner Emma Dazeley who challenged Jake. Suffice to say Jake fled leaving sufficient evidence allowing him to be identified and was, subsequently, jailed for two years. Emma was awarded £500 for her courage and determination for tackling the intruder. Sadly Emma wanted to share her award with Charlie but he flew off and has not returned.

2020 – Krugersdorp – South Africa

The following case brings to mind Michael Caine's famous line from *The Italian Job: 'You were only supposed to blow the bloody doors off.'* Robbers targeted a security van which was packed with bank notes but used an excess of dynamite and managed to blow off all four sides and the roof of the van. Videos have emerged of passers-by stuffing scattered notes into bags and pockets. The gang escaped with as much money as they could gather from the cash confetti.

2020 – Marseilles – France

Three men who had, clearly, been advised of a delivery of valuable jewellery to the upmarket Printemps La Valentine store. They fired shots in the air and set fire to the security van to force crew out of the vehicle. However, it transpired they had managed to steal £5,000 worth of costume jewellery while failing to spot the £500,000 of valuable gems.

2020 – Swindon – England

Frederick Moulton was attempting to burgle a house in Swindon. However he got jammed in a window when his leg got stuck and ended up suspended upside down and was forced to phone the emergency services to be released.

2020 – Slovenia

Julija Adlesic agreed with her boyfriend to sever her left hand above the wrist in the hope of claiming £700,000. However investigators discovered Julija and her boyfriend had signed contracts with five different insurance companies the year before and her boyfriend had also spent time seeking information about how artificial hands worked. The boyfriend was sentenced to three years in prison, Julija to two years and the boyfriend's father received a one year suspended sentence. The severed hand was recovered and reattached.

2020 – Parkhurst Prison – Isle of Wight – England

A serving prisoner has been charged with selling urine to two fellow inmates. I have no further comment to make.

2021 – Staffordshire – England

During a burglary one of the criminals sat on his phone and unknowingly called emergency operators who concluded that what was happening was suspicious. The call was tracked and officers were able to listen to the break-in right up to the point they could hear the sirens arrive at the house.

Two males were arrested: one was 49 and another 42. A Chief Inspector tweeted: *'I think we just arrested the world's unluckiest burglars.'*

2021 – St Petersburg – Russia

I don't think listing this case under Incompetent Criminals is fair. A former commander in the Russian Navy, unnamed, has been charged with stealing 13-tonne bronze propellers from the destroyer, *Bespokoyny,* between 2016 and 2018 and replacing them with propellers made from cheaper material. How on earth do you steal 13-tonne metal objects without anyone noticing?

Just to put the matter in context Russian prosecutors stated in 2019 there were more than 10,000 cases of bribery, theft or embezzlement uncovered.

2021 – Slovakia

A man tried to rob a petrol station in Bratislava. He hit an employee, took the cash register and then demanded money from the safe. However a Czech woman then distracted him by performing a 'sex act' until the police arrived!

2021 – Germany/France

In 2012 a burglar broke into five flats in the town of Gevelsberg, Germany. He stole jewellery and sports bags amongst other things. However at one crime scene he left a half-eaten sausage from which the police extracted DNA which was then uploaded to an international database.

In February 2021 the French police uploaded DNA from a crime scene which matched that uploaded from Germany in 2012. The miscreant is a 30-year-old Albanian and for him things have taken a turn for the 'wurst.'

2021 – Gloucester – England

Judge Ian Lawrie QC described three burglars, David Newman, Mark Rabjohns and Peter Fitzharris as: '... *three buffoons with utter incompetence in carrying out this burglary.'* Briefly they had broken into the Cheltenham Tweed Company shop with the intention of drilling into Promenade Antiques next door. They managed to bring down a party wall and activate an alarm. They ran off into the winter night dressed in T-shirts and pants. They were quickly arrested.

2021 – Bicester – England

Sarah White arrived back at her home in Bicester to discover she had been burgled. Jewellery had been stolen and, in addition, her African grey parrot called Sky had also been taken. Now Sky, by her owner's own admission, is a nasty piece of work. She shrieks 'come on' before biting. Sings 'do, do, do' repeatedly. Mostly she hates men. She cannot fly very well and walks everywhere. The precise reasons are not known but suffice to say after a month Sky was returned to her owner.

2021 – England

Alan Slattery, 67, of St Leonards on Sea, was trying to rob a bank but the cashiers could not read his handwriting. After being caught he received a four-year jail sentence.

2021 – Alicante – Spain

An unnamed Italian attempted to rob the Banco Sabadell in Alicante. Customers and staff quickly realised they could overpower him because the gun he was using was obviously fake. During the struggle his false leg fell off, after which the robber surrendered.

2021 – Suffolk – England

A bungling fuel thief attempted to siphon the petrol from a motor home. The police were called when the motorhome owners heard screams and someone being sick. The thief had siphoned the contents of the motorhome toilet into his mouth!

Italy

To avoid misunderstandings I should explain I like Italy and Italians but they do, sometimes, produce some glorious cases.

2008 – Sampierdarena – Italy

Alvaro Perez, originally from Ecuador, conducted dental operations on hundreds of patients over many years despite having no qualifications whatsoever. His dental equipment included a screwdriver, mallet and household pliers. Eventually one patient complained of the excruciating pain he had endured. Alvaro was arrested for practicing without a licence.

2008 – Sicily – Italy

Danilo Giuffida is gay. He was summoned to attend for compulsory National Service. The Military Authorities concluded, since he was gay, he was disabled from serving in the armed forces. When Danilo applied for a driving licence it was issued but with a stamp indicating Danilo was disabled and thus would need to be re-examined every twelve months. Danilo objected, sued the Italian state and won €100,000.

2015 – Palermo – Italy

Three women complained their employer had acted inappropriately by touching their private parts. The Court concluded '... *the conduct was playful, driven by an imma-ture sense of humour*!' The Court also decided an unwanted kiss on the neck is not sexual harassment since the neck is not an erogenous zone.

2016 – Latina – Italy

Using section 572 of the Italian Penal Code, one house-wife could potentially face six years in prison for failing to keep a tidy house, for not placing meals on the table and generally being slovenly. She was reported by her husband to the local police who referred the matter to the judiciary.

2016 – Bellavista di Trivero – Italy

Pierangelo Bussolera had a mother who was elderly and very popular. She sat on her balcony waving to passers-by and gossiping to neighbours. Then one day she no longer appeared and the neighbours became suspicious. The matter was reported to the police who arranged to visit Pierangelo. It transpired the old lady had died and had been kept in the deep freeze. Her death had not been re-ported so her son could continue collecting various bene-fits. He had recently retrieved his mother from her frozen tomb. The problem was she had not defrosted by the time the police arrived.

2019 – San Donà di Piave – Italy

Alberto Vazzoler, who is officially unemployed and penniless, had three homes, two motor yachts and a fleet of luxury cars, was accused of laundering more than €46 million for people across Europe. It transpired during his trial that his partner, Ms. Moro, had baked a strudel in an oven he used to hide cash amounting to €40,000, all of which went up in smoke. Could this be the world's most expensive pudding?

15

JUDICIAL PRONOUNCEMENTS

The following are interesting, in my view, because of what they say about the way society has changed over the years.

1867 – England

In the case of Regina v Norwood in 1867 Judge Blackburn concluded: *'A man's home is where his wife is.'* Quite right too.

A MAN'S HOME IS HIS WIFE'S CASTLE.

1933 – England

Lord Justice Greer – *'A reasonable man takes magazines at home and in the evening pushes the lawn mower in his shirt sleeves.'*

1947 – England

A judge concluded a husband who wanted to make love after every meal was unreasonable.

1960 – England

The case was concerned with whether the book 'Lady Chatterley's Lover' by D H Lawrence was obscene. Technically R v Penguin Books Ltd (1961) Crim LR 176. Prosecuting Counsel made the following statement to the jury:

'... ask yourself the question when you read it through: would you approve of your young sons, young daughters – because girls can read as well as boys – reading this book? Is it a book you would even wish your wife or servants to read?'

It is my view Lawrence is a grossly overrated writer and the book is tedious but the above showed just how far out of touch some people in the Legal Profession were with the ordinary members of the jury.

1971 – England

In York Crown Court in the trial of Philip McCutcheon, who had been arrested for the twentieth time after driving a getaway car, this time into two parked vans, he was offered the following advice by Judge Percy:

'May I advise you that I really think you should give burglary up. You have a withered hand, an artificial leg and only one eye. You have been caught in Otley, Leeds, Harrogate, Norwich, Beverley, Hull and York. How can you succeed? You are a rotten burglar. You are always being caught.'

1976 – England

Judge Sutcliffe, while presiding over a rape trial observed:

'It is well known that women in particular and small boys are liable to be untruthful and invent stories.'

1980 – England

The Court of Appeal concluded making love once a week was reasonable as long as it lasted for at least 240 seconds!

2003 – England

Lord Justice Lewison in a copyright case involving Ant'ill Mob and Heartless Crew stated:

'It is a faintly surreal experience for three gentlemen in horsehair wigs examining the meaning of such phrases as "mish mish man" and "shizzle my nizzle."'

2012 – Wales

Judge Manning-Davies fined a man £200 for urinating in public:

'*This isn't France you know where that sort of behaviour is acceptable.*'

I have spent some time in Nantes and have some sympathy with the observations of the Judge.

2016 – India

The High Court Judgement in the State of Himachal Pradesh, India was as follows:

'*However, the learned counsel... cannot derive the fullest succour from the aforesaid acquiescence... given its sinew suffering partial dissipation from an imminent display occurring in the impugned pronouncement hereat wherewithin unravelments are held qua the rendition recorded by the learned Rent Controller...*'

The Judgement continued:

'*The summum bonum of the aforesaid discussion is that all the aforesaid material which existed before learned Executing Court standing slighted besides their impact standing*' *untenably undermined by him whereupon the ensuing sequel therefrom is of the learned Executing Court while pronouncing its impugned rendition overlooking the relevant and germane evidence besides its not appreciating its worth. Consequently the order impugned suffers from a gross absurdity and perversity of misappreciation of material on record.'*

Well I hope that's clear! If the decision means nothing to you then you are not alone. The Supreme Court in India dismissed the judgement as gibberish and directed it be redrafted because it was simply unintelligible.

Judicial Humour: Ireland 1880's

Lord Justice Holmes sentenced an elderly man to 15 years in prison. The man exclaimed:

'I shan't live that long.'

The Judge responded:

'Well do the best you can.'

16

MISCELLANEOUS

This, as the title suggests, is a collection of cases which don't fit easily into any other category apart from the fact they appeal to my rather disordered mind.

1992 – Richest Dog in the World

In 1992 Countess Karlotta Liebenstein died leaving, in her will, some $65 million to her dog Gunther III who has since died. Gunther IV inherited from his father and the amount held in trust for him is $375 million making Gunther IV the richest dog and probably the richest animal in the world.

2013 – Liverpool – England

Neil McArdle was due to get married. The great day arrived and he realised he had forgotten to book the Register Office. The solution to his problem, he decided, was to phone in a bomb threat thus the Register Office would be closed and the marriage would have to be postponed. The call was traced and Mr. McArdle spent some time in prison providing a further reason to delay the marriage.

2015 – Dusseldorf – Germany

There have been some attempts in recent times to make it illegal for men to stand in order to urinate. See, for example, a proposal by the Swedish Left Part in Sormland County Council.

A landlord in Dusseldorf sought damages of £1,400 because he claimed his marble floors had been damaged by urine. Judge Stefan Hank concluded:

'Despite growing domestication of men in this matter urinating while standing up is still common practice.'

2017 – Japan

A former car worker aged 50 died after a 6-ton pile of pornography which he had accumulated collapsed on top of him. Every space in his flat was filled with heaps of magazines. His body was only discovered after six months when the landlord called to find why the rent had not been paid.

2018 – Pilar –Argentina

Investigators found 540kg of marijuana missing from a police warehouse in Pilar. The former police commissioner, a Mr. Specia, and fellow officers told the judge the drugs had been eaten by mice. The judge concluded, after taking expert advice, the mice would not have mistaken the drug for food and, if they had, a lot of mice corpses would have been found.

2018 – Alberta – Canada

A man in Alberta changed the gender marking on his birth certificate and other government ID from male to female in order to obtain cheaper car insurance.

2019 – Kentucky – USA

Certain welders wanted to highlight how inadequate the American Welding Society standards were thus they filed bids for three dogs called Robert Dash, Adam Barker and Henry Wolfe to be certified, all of which passed. The result is the State Legislators in Kentucky will vote on House Bill 239 which will stop canines becoming registered welders.

2019 – Moscow – Russia

A naked man was arrested in Moscow after trying to board a plane while shouting his clothes made him less agile and aerodynamic. Witnesses said he passed through checks at the airport before stripping naked and running from the terminal to the aircraft.

2019 – England

Kent County Council forced The Whole Earth Company to withdraw a product called '3 Nut Butter', which, on the label, makes it plain it contains walnuts, pecans and peanuts, because it does not include a 'nut allergy' warning in English. This has prompted a number of comments including:

'If anyone eats this and doesn't realise it has nuts then I am afraid it's called natural selection.'

and

'Are people so stupid they need to be told that 3 Nut Butter contains nuts?'

2019 – Ohio – USA

A disgruntled customer in Perkins Restaurant, Painesville pulled an iguana from under his shirt and threw it at the manager of the diner. He was arrested for disorderly conduct. The iguana was unharmed.

2019 – Stockport – England

An 81-year-old lady has been banned from wearing a bikini inside her home if she is near windows!

2019 – Cardiff – Wales

Thomas Bower entered the Brewdog Bar in Cardiff and ordered a bottle of Pink IPA which was for sale at £4. He was informed by the staff this was for women only since it had been launched to highlight the gender pay gap. He was advised he could order the Punk IPA which was £5. In order to get the less expensive drink Mr. Bower identified himself as female and was served Pink IPA. Mr. Bower sued the Brewdog Brewery for sex discrimination and was awarded £1000 which he has given to charity.

(As a matter of interest the University and College Union has announced that they have a long history of enabling members to self-identify '... whether that is being black, disabled, LGBT or women.'

A man recently obtained an Art Council Grant reserved for ethnic minorities, despite the fact he had two Irish parents, because he claimed he was a 'born again African' who had gone 'through the struggles of the black man.')

2019 – France – Various

France has, some might say, fairly curious laws as they relate to pensions entitlements. For example it was recently disclosed thirty 'employees' had continued to receive salaries even though their jobs has been abolished in 1989, over thirty years ago. In addition the 'General Director of Services' for the town of Sainte-Savine had, over ten years, received £450,000 for doing absolutely nothing at all.

2019 – France – Definition of work accidents

In 2017 the French Courts decided that an executive of a French company who was off duty and fell while dancing in a disco in China at 2 a.m. and injured his wrist had suffered a workplace injury.

In another case a man referred to as 'Xavier X', a married man with two children, while on assignment in Paris in 2013 met and had sex with a woman who was not his wife. Shortly afterwards he was found dead from a heart attack. The French courts have decided this is also a workplace accident or an *accident du travail*. The lawyers for the employer on appeal, which failed, asserted that Xavier was 'not performing duties for his employer when he suffered his heart attack.' One can only speculate what duties he was performing. The consequence of the decision is that the partner and children of Xavier would receive significant benefits including 80% of Xavier's salary until his normal retirement age and then a share of his pension.

2019 – Castro Urdiales – Spain

Jesus Maria Baranda disappeared and in order to try to discover some evidence of his whereabouts the police decided to search the house occupied by him and his partner Maria Del Carmen Merino. Ms. Merino gave a box to her friend asking her to keep it because it contained sex toys and Ms.

Merino would be embarrassed if the police discovered it. After becoming aware of a peculiar smell coming from the box the friend opened it only to discover various sex toys and a decomposed head. Ms. Merino has been arrested. Mr. Baranda disappeared in February.

Excuses for not filling your United Kingdom tax return

The following excuses have been provided to Her Majesty's Revenue and Customs:

My mother-in-law is a witch and put a curse on them;

They were too short to reach the post box;

and

My boiler broke so I was too cold to type.

17

THE MOON, SUN, GOD, SATAN AND PASTAFARIANISM

1971 – Pennsylvania – USA

Gerald Mayo sued 'Satan and his staff' for causing his downfall by the infliction of misery and the placing of obstacles in his path. Satan refused to give evidence apparently.

1980 – California – USA

Dennis Hope, a used car salesman, registered ownership of the Moon. He declared himself *'... the omniscient ruler of the lunar surface'* with the title 'Head Cheese.' He sold lots to six million people and made $11,000,000.

2005 – Romania

Pavel M was convicted for murder. He sued God for breach of contract since God had not kept the promises made at his christening. God did not make an appearance.

2008 – Montana – USA

Jason Indreland said his rights as a Satanist had been denied while in prison. He issued proceedings for $10 million. He settled for $50 and the promise of a review.

Pastafarianism

This is a religion attached to the church of the 'Flying Spaghetti Monster.' It proposes the world was created by airborne spaghetti and meatball-based human beings and that humans evolved from pirates.

They don't say 'Amen,' they say 'Ramen,' a tribute to Japanese Noodles. Ministers are called 'Ministeroni.' They have applied for and have become an official religion in Poland.

And in 2016 the Church of the Flying Spaghetti Monster was also recognized as a religion in the Netherlands. They refer to themselves as 'pastafarians.' Their faith is expressed by putting a colander on their heads. Services are devoted to socialising so they eat pasta, drink beer and discuss faith. Heaven is a beer volcano with a 'stripper factory.'

In 2016 the first Pastafarian wedding was held in New Zealand:

18

STRANGE
AFFECTIONS

There is something glorious about the unpredictability of human behaviour but it can be incomprehensible as these cases, hopefully, demonstrate.

1993 – Karl Watkins – Redditch – England

Karl was charged with five counts of 'outraging public decency' while trying to have sex with a pavement. He claimed it was a case of mistaken identity. In 1995 he was back in court for simulating sex with black plastic bin liners. He spent nights on rubbish piles and had been found in wheelie bins. The court ordered a psychiatric assessment!

2007 – Robert Stewart – Ayr – Scotland

Robert Stewart aged 51 was (and is) a sexual cyclist. He was caught, naked from the waist down, stimulating sex with his cycle by cleaners in his hostel room. He admitted sexual breach of the peace and was placed on probation.

2008 – Wiltshire

A man was arrested in Westbury Wiltshire for engaging in sexual activity with a lamp post. I really cannot think of anything to add.

2017 – Florin Grosu – Romford

Draped in a dressing gown at 11.00 a.m. Florin was seen being intimate with a drainage cover. A somewhat unyielding surface you may imagine. He was remanded in custody after pleading guilty to the offence.

2019 – Wigan – England

Mr. Trevor Smith was caught by staff at Wigan Station with his pants around his ankles attempting to be intimate with a plastic traffic cone. He received a suspended sentence but was spared prison.

Emotional Support Animals

People who have found flying stressful or emotional have been allowed to bring pets to help them. These have included:

A pig, which in fact had to be removed because of its unfortunate toilet habits.

A duck, called Mr. Stinkerbutt.

and

A very large dalmatian dog, a peacock, turkey, a small horse etc.

19

TRAFFIC OFFENCES

2018 – Wareham – England

A motorcycle and a Warrior tank were involved in a collision. The motor cyclist was taken to Poole Hospital for treatment with a suspected fractured arm. The driver of the tank was uninjured! The police appealed for witnesses to the accident.

2019 – Kingsbridge – England

The Police were called to an accident on the road between Marlborough and Kingsbridge in Devon about three miles from the sea. They found a car overturned in a ditch. The driver advised he had swerved to avoid an octopus! After a comprehensive search the police could find no trace of the offending sea creature and charged the man with driving while under the influence of drugs.

2019 – North Lincolnshire – England

The driver of Range Rover carrying two young children was stopped after recording a speed of 118 miles per hour. His excuse was he was speeding because of a smelly nappy.

2019 – Bavaria – Germany

A man was stopped by police for driving erratically on a motorway. He was found to have a kangaroo, two Siberian owls, six barnacle geese and ten ducks in the car. The man advised he was a vet, had bought the animals in the Netherlands and was taking them to Poland for breeding. A police spokesman said:

'A kangaroo free inside a car – that's an unusual occurrence. If someone swerves about on the road we tend to think about alcohol not half a petting zoo in the car.'

The transport of live animals in cars would appear to a problem for the German police who recently stopped in a man in Hesse who was carrying a cow in his Seat Inca minivan.

2019 – Marlow – England

A van driver was stopped by the police who discovered a foot well so full of rubbish it was dangerous. He was fined £500 and had points put on his license.

2019 – Newbury – England

A man was fined £100 for careless driving, after staying in the middle lane of the M4 motorway for some miles despite the fact that the left-hand lane was entirely clear.

You can also be charged with careless driving for driving too slowly on a motorway because that leads to undertaking, tailgating, congestion and road rage.

20

THE LAW – AN INTRODUCTION

Introduction

I am a 'legal geek' and once spent much time writing 'worthy' papers for other 'worthy legal geeks' to read. As some sort of relaxation I have accumulated material from various sources which I thought would be suitable to include in the annual printed perambulations I have compiled. I then imposed them on non-legal geeks whether they liked them or not. Often I asked the recipients if they enjoyed my 'gift' and watched for the 'rictus' smile when they said: 'Yes of course. I look forward to next year's.'

In this section I have tried to 'spread my wings.' I have, of course, included matters 'legal' which have caught my attention but, in addition, other material which has made me smile or think.

To quote Oscar Wilde:

'I write because it gives me the greatest possible pleasure to write. If my work pleases the few, I am gratified.'

As before the subjects included are an arbitrary choice. The only thing they have in common is that I find them interesting and/or amusing.

I have long since recognized that while the law is a passion for me, the legal world often ranks with estate agents and politicians as the profession most distrusted by the general public. So once again I shall begin with some anti-lawyer quotes to get us all in the mood.

'A multiplicity of laws is a sign of bad government.'

Aristotle

St Ivo Helory of Kermarton

Let me admit an interest. I am a fan of Saint Ivo. He was born in Brittany in 1253 and is one of the Catholic patron saints of lawyers. (Another is Saint Sir Thomas More.) Even during his lifetime St Ivo was regarded as remarkable. A folk verse went:

'St Ivo was a Breton and a lawyer but not a thief, a remarkable thing in people's eyes.' (I know it doesn't scan well but it was probably much more poetic in the original Breton.)

There is a story that when St Ivo reached heaven several nuns arrived on the same day. St Peter said the nuns could not enter 'because we have many nuns in heaven.' However, when St Ivo arrived St Peter said: 'You may enter. We don't have a single lawyer here now.'

'The first thing we do, let's kill all lawyers.'

Shakespeare – Henry VI, Part 2, Act IV Scene 2, (1591)

'Laws are like cobwebs, which may catch small flies, but let wasps and hornets break through.'

Jonathan Swift: 'A tale of tub' (1704)

Mrs. Bertram: That sounds like nonsense, my dear.

Mr. Bertram: May be so my dear; but it may be very good law for all that.

Sir Walter Scott: 'Guy Mannering' chapter 9 (1815)

'Laws are like sausages – it is best not to see them being made.'

Misattributed to Bismark and more accurately attributed to John Godfrey Saxe (1869)

'The majestic egalitarianism of the law, which forbids rich and poor alike to sleep under bridges, to beg in streets, and to steal bread'

Anatole France: 'Le Lys Rouge' chapter 7 (1894)

'I would not take libel proceedings if it were stated that I had killed my grandmother and eaten her.'

William Thomas Stead (Newspaper editor sadly lost in the Titanic Disaster 1912)

'In a British courtroom an ordinary act like eating a sausage can be made under cross-examination to sound like some bizarre perversion.'

Auberon Waugh

'There's no certainty in the law, it's a complete will-o'-the wisp.'

Lord Denning (Former Lord Justice of Appeal and Master of the Rolls)

I once practiced as a 'private client lawyer' and dealt with a lot of estates so I find the following particularly apposite:

'The only way you can beat the lawyers is to die with nothing.'

Will Rogers (American actor 1879-1935).

(In my experience to die leaving debts is even more effective. I can assure you you will be remembered.)

'You cannot live without lawyers and you certainly cannot die without them.'

Joseph Choate (USA Lawyer and Diplomat).

Quite right. We all have a living to earn.

'Death is the most convenient time to tax rich people.'

David Lloyd George (UK Prime Minister 1916 – 1922)

An excess of law

There are over 12,000 offences under English law including disturbing a pack of eggs when directed not to do so by an authorised officer, selling or offering to sell game birds which have been shot on a Sunday (how would you know?) and swimming on the wreck of the Titanic (which is 12,600 feet below the surface of the Atlantic Ocean.)

21

MORE MISCELLANEOUS

Writing – 3400 BC/3200 BC

This is rather depressing (at least I think so) but it is now thought writing was first used to give receipts and record debts.

How many commandments are there in the Bible?

We are used to the idea that there are Ten Commandments even if we cannot name them all. In fact there are thirteen, nineteen or possibly 613. Exodus 20 and Deuteronomy 5 make it clear there are more than ten: indeed thirteen. There then follow a further six with regard to your neighbour's possessions which, you are exhorted, thou shalt not covet. Making nineteen so far. But based on the book of Leviticus, Orthodox Judaism asserts there are in fact 613 commandments breaking down into 248 'thou shalts' and 365 'thou shalt nots.'

Pope Benedict IX (circa 1012 – 1056)

Pope Benedict IX (born Theophylactus of Tusculum) holds the record for being the youngest Pope ever. Some say he became Pope at age 12, others at age 20 and any number in between. But he is the only man who became Pope on more than one occasion and the only man to have sold the papacy. He was first Pope from 1032-1044 then again in 1045 and finally from 1047-1048. In 1045 he sold the papacy to Joan Gratian who then succeeded him as Gregory VI.

10 Downing Street

Apropos of nothing at all, just because it amuses me, the last private owner of 10 Downing Street was called Mr. Chicken! (The title Prime Minister was only officially recognised in 1905.)

1830

On 15 September 1830 the Liverpool and Manchester Railway was opened as the first inter-city railway in the world. William Huskinsson, a former MP and member of the Cabinet, was determined to ingratiate himself with the then Prime Minister, the Duke of Wellington. He was hanging around on the track when a train approached from the opposite direction. Huskinsson ignored the warnings and was killed. And thus became the first casualty of a train accident.

Nineteenth century – Charles Dickens – Bleak House

Those familiar with Dickens's Bleak House will know of the fictional case of *Jarndyce v Jarndyce*. (Frankly I have always found Dickens unbelievably dull.) However, Dickens almost certainly got his inspiration from the case of *Jennens v Jennens* which commenced in 1798 and was abandoned in 1915 (after 117 years) when the legal fees had eaten the entire estate.

1897 – Paris – Who first wore a medical face mask?

In these days of COVID and debates about the effectiveness of face masks it is interesting to note the first doctor to wear a mask, made from six layers of gauze, was Paul Berger in 1897. He was persuaded to adopt the practice after reading the work of Doctor Carl Flugge who revealed that saliva is such a good breeding ground for bacteria. The wearing of medical masks gradually became common practice.

1985 – Oklahoma City – USA

Dennis Newton was on trial for armed robbery. The supervisor of the store was asked to identify the culprit at which point he indicated Dennis. The defendant leapt to his feet, accused the witness of lying and stated: 'I should have blown your f****** head off.' After a moment of silence Dennis added: 'If I'd been the one there.' Dennis was sentenced to thirty years.

1991 – Tucson – USA

Jean Paul Barrett was serving a 33-year prison sentence for forgery and fraud. He escaped from jail by a having a forged release order faxed to prison authorities.

1993 – Oxford – England

Two patrol officers stopped a father and son for not wearing seat belts. An argument broke out at which point reinforcements were summoned. The defence lawyer pointed out: 'It should not have taken 21 officers, a helicopter and a heavily armed squad to question two men over a traffic offence.' The charges were dismissed.

1994 – Florida – USA

Michael Mufford, serving time for burglary and theft, escaped from Gainesville Work Camp, Florida by riding a lawnmower into the nearby woods.

1997 – England

In 2020 Sir Roger Penrose was awarded the Nobel Prize for physics. However, in 1997 it transpired that Kleenex had made toilet tissue embossed with a mathematical tiling system Sir Roger had designed. (Before anyone asks, I have no idea what a mathematical tiling system is.) He sued and won.

A spokesman said:

'When it comes to the population of Great Britain being invited by a multinational to wipe their bottoms on the work of a knight of the realm without his permission then a last stand must be made.'

Quite right. Standards must be maintained!

1998 – England – London

Three young men were accused of stealing three cans of lager worth £1.80. After a trial costing £131,000 the judge dismissed the case for lack of evidence.

2003 – Oxford – England

Sam Brown was somebody else who had imbibed well but not wisely during a night out to celebrate after his final exams. He said to a police officer: *'Excuse me. Do you realise your horse is gay?'* He was arrested under the Public Order Act 1986 for making homophobic remarks likely to cause alarm and distress and, since he refused to pay an £80 fine, spent a night in a police cell. When he was brought up in front of the Magistrates it transpired the Crown Prosecution service had chosen, sensibly you may think, to discontinue the case.

2011 – Shropshire – England

This is included because yet again the headline which appeared in the Shropshire Star in 2011 is just too good to ignore: 'Flatulent Shropshire dentist found guilty of misconduct.' The details behind the headline are as follows.

Matthew Walton is a dentist who worked for the Green End Dental Practice in Whitchurch. He 'found it funny' to break wind next to colleagues having lunch and in front of patients. He also belched and used swear words and had a lack of respect for the elderly and disabled. He was found guilty of 'unprofessional and inappropriate behaviour.' Well, how surprising is that?

2016 – United Kingdom

In 2012 Maythem al-Ansari was on bail and facing jail over a multi-million-pound mortgage fraud. Despite that he persuaded the Home Office to give him a new passport and he promptly fled to Syria. In 2016 he voluntarily returned to the United Kingdom on the basis that being in prison in the UK was preferable to living in a war zone.

2019 – Rotterdam – Holland

The police were called to an incident in which it was reported a man, who was on probation, was making threats with weapons and possibly carrying a firearm. The officers attended and discovered no weapons were involved but there was an argument between a man and his ex-partner.

Nevertheless the police decided the man was in breach of the terms of his conditional release and decided he should be taken back into custody. The man presented a Monopoly 'Get out of Jail Free' card and asked if he could use it that one time. The police appreciated the originality but returned him to jail anyway.

2019 – Perth – Australia

The police were called after neighbours heard a man screaming: *'WHY WON'T YOU DIE?'* It turned out the man suffered from extreme arachnophobia and his anger was directed at a spider. The spider did, indeed, eventually die.

2019 – Erfurt – Germany

A raccoon got drunk after drinking unfinished glasses of mulled wine and passed out under a bin. It was shot by a local hunter. The police said it was *'obviously intoxicated.'* I would have thought a strong cup of black coffee and a night in the cells would have been sufficient.

2019 – England

A charity has asked for the Dangerous Wild Animals Act 1976 be updated since, after research, they have discovered the following animals are being kept by ordinary members of the public and not in zoos: 'An elephant in Wales, in England a giraffe, fourteen wolves, three bears, thirteen leopards, three cheetahs, nine lions and nine tigers. Other species kept include zebras, camels and otters.'

2019 – Salisbury – England

Keith Cutler is a Resident Judge in Salisbury. He was summoned for jury service and pointed out he was due to be the judge on the trial in question. His appeal was rejected and he was informed he would need to apply to the Resident Judge. He explained, patiently, that he *was* the Resident Judge.

2019 – Rio de Janeiro – Brazil

Maria Schiave had failed her driving test on a number of occasions so her son, Heitor Marcio Schiave, a car mechanic, decided to take it on her behalf. He dressed as his mother and applied copious make up. However the driving examiner, Aline Mendonca, became suspicious and the deceit was discovered. A judge advised that even if the attempted fraud had not been discovered Heitor would not have passed since his parallel parking was dreadful. Heitor faces a fine and a possible prison sentence.

2019 – Utah – USA

The following story resonates with me since it involves a notary.

Jeanne Souron-Mathers, aged 75, was found dead in her home after the police were called to conduct a welfare check since she had not been heard from for two weeks. Jeanne's death was thought to be from natural causes. However in searching the house they found the body of Paul Mathers, her late husband, in the deep freeze. It would appear he had been dead for some ten years. The suggestion is Jeanne had concealed his death so she could continue to claim various welfare payments.

What was odd is that the police found a 'notarised' letter signed by Paul which said his wife was not responsible for his death. The notary stated she had not read the letter before notarising it. So that's OK then.

2019 – North Carolina – USA

Mr. Thomas and Mrs. Elisa Milam of Lewisville, North Carolina, were watching a film in bed when they became aware of a noise downstairs. Mr. Thomas, who is ex-military, prepared to confront the intruder but first he called the police. The officers burst through the front door and then, after a short time, called Mr. Thomas asking him to put down any weapons he may have and come downstairs. An officer asked 'Is this your Roomba?' It transpired that the Roomba, a robotic vacuum cleaner, had somehow turned itself on and was cleaning the house but had got stuck in the hall.

2020 – Plymouth – England

Paul Elcombe had an altercation with another customer, Kyle Towers, in a café in Plymouth. He gave vent to his frustration by throwing a seagull at his antagonist. He denies wounding with intent to cause grievous bodily harm.

He has yet to enter a plea to the charge of injuring a wild bird.

2020 – United Kingdom – Commuting for work

Beggars have been 'commuting' between Glasgow and Carlisle since in Scotland aggressive begging carries a penalty of up to a year in prison and a £5,000 fine while in England and Wales the maximum fine is £1,000.

2020 – Arizona – USA

A 62-year-old driver was caught trying to disguise a fake skeleton as a passenger in his car so he could use the high occupancy vehicle lane. The driver was pulled over when an official 'noticed' the skeleton which was wearing a hat and was tied to the passenger seat with yellow rope.

2020 – Germany

The police in Germany are having to deal with a growing nuisance. As an example of this new problem a couple in Gebenach, Bavaria, were shocked to discover a pair of legs poking out from under a woollen rug under a road bridge. It turned out to be a life-sized 'sex doll' made of lifelike

latex. (It appears the sex doll industry has developed since
the days of the inflatable variety.) The latex versions are
very realistic (so I am told!) and disposal is not easy. The
consequence is that, for example, sightings in canals and
rivers have often prompted particularly elaborate salvage
operations. Recently on the River Elbe the emergency services were called out to retrieve a body. It turned out to be
a 'doll' packed into a box with its feet poking out.

2020 – Canada – Life imitating Art

Michael Davy, from British Columbia, sued Akhtar Kid-
wai, a breeder of parrots, after he purchased an eclectus
parrot called Tiberius for £1,200. Normally this breed
of parrot lives for 30/40 years but this bird, while not
dead, was almost dead. When Mr. Davey noticed the bird
was missing a few tail feathers he was informed 'the bird
was moulting and had clipped wings but was otherwise
healthy.' To paraphrase John Cleese the plumage did not
enter into it. It turned out the poor bird had 'psittacine
beak and feather disease,' whatever that is. Tiberius is likely
to be an ex-parrot within a short time but has not yet
joined the 'choir invisible.' Mr Davey has received a 75%
refund and his vet fees.

2020 – Rome - Italy

Davad Zukanovic and his cousin Lil Ahmetovic were serving a jail sentence and were due to be released 2029. They escaped from prison after sawing through the bars of their cell, used a fire hose to scale a wall and then used bolt cutters to get through a wire fence. However, they left a polite note saying they had to attend to a family matter and would return when the issue had been resolved. The prison authorities are sceptical they will keep their promise!

2020 – Kew Palace

Rachel Mackay, a manager for Historic Royal Palaces, each year takes a deep sigh when a familiar brown envelope arrives addressed to 'The Current Occupier, Kew Palace.' The palace has not been occupied for two centuries. To quote Rachel: 'Oh good. It's the time of year where I have to explain to the TV Licensing Authority why George III has not paid his TV licence since 1820.'

2020 – Spain

I am quite certain the incidence of those in prison who self-harm is no greater or less in Spain than elsewhere. However, a couple of particular examples have come to light. In a prison near Badajoz on 26 September a prisoner was found to have cut off his earlobes and eaten them.

In a prison near Cadiz, an inmate named Puerto III cut off his penis after he discovered his wife had refused a conjugal visit.

2021 – Paris – France

Police broke up an orgy in a warehouse near Paris and charged 81 people with breaching curfew restrictions. A policeman said: *'... there were also problems with social distancing!'*

2021 – London – England

This is by way of a cautionary tale. In the case of Beattie Passive Norse Ltd and Another v Canham Consulting Beattie Passive claimed £3.7 million damages. Canham had offered £50,000 to settle the matter and later increased the offer to £110,000. Beattie Passive declined to accept and the matter went to trial. Beattie Passive won and were awarded £2,000 in damages and also ordered to pay £495,000 in legal costs!

2021 – London – England – A very curious democracy

The late Tony Benn (1925-2014) was a Member of Parliament for Bristol South East and later Chesterfield. When his father died in 1960 he inherited the title Viscount Stansgate. That meant he could no longer continue as a M.P. He campaigned, successfully, to be allowed to renounce the title which resulted in the Peerage Act 1963. He once said: *'Why would you want your teeth drilled by someone who was not a dentist but whose father was?'*

Tony Blair embarked on an incomplete reform of the House of Lords in 1999 by which most hereditary peers no longer had an automatic right to sit in the House of Lords but, as a concession, agreed 92 hereditary peers could continue to sit subject to elections. Stephen Benn, the eldest son of Tony Benn has resumed the title of Viscount Stansgate and won an 'election' to be one of the hereditary Labour Peers in the House of Lords. There were only three electors and he was the only candidate! One can only speculate at what his father would have said.

2021 – England

Oli London, a 'social influencer', I really don't know, 'came out' as a 'non-binary person.' I don't know what that means either but am assured it is not, of itself, noteworthy in the modern world. What is remarkable is that Oli has come out as a Korean. He loves Korean culture and has had extensive surgery to his face and has announced he wishes to be known as Korean. It has been decided, apparently, that a man may become a woman and vice versa simply by saying so but changing your ethnicity is altogether more problematic. The reaction to his announcement has not been greeted with universal acclamation.

2021 – Los Angeles – USA

A man in Los Angeles identified as 'trans' in order to get into a women's changing room in a spa and wave his male private parts at the women in the changing room. A number of women demonstrated against such activities. 'Antifa' activists then assaulted the demonstrators. ('Antifa' is a movement against racism and fascism.) It seems if you are against fascism that means you can beat up women who don't want male private parts flashed at them in spa changing rooms. Strange world!

2021 Stoke England

From Stoke's *The Sentinel* is a report of a Staffordshire solicitor, Iain Haley, pleading for clemency for his client

Stephen Cooper, 45, who had stolen a packet of Viagra from a pharmacy. He asserted: 'He is not a hardened criminal.' I have nothing to add.

Mortality

I am advised by my youngest son, Robert of that ilk, another collector of inconsequential facts, that in one year in the United Kingdom ninety-nine people were killed in falls from beds, fifty-two in falls from chairs, 655 from falling down stairs, five from bee stings and thirty-five from drowning in baths. (Actually the latest figures show a decline in the drowning in the bath situation with only twenty-nine losing their life in this way.) There were in one year in the UK 181,000 accidents resulting in physical injury of which 1,792 were fatal. Of those fatalities 107 were cyclists. The World Health Organisation calculate 1.25 million people worldwide die in road traffic accidents each year.

Royal Appointments

The Monarch appoints many people to the Royal Household including an Astronomer, a Hereditary Carver (no one has the faintest idea what the Hereditary Carver does)

and a Sculptor in Ordinary. In addition there is a Crown
Equerry who handles the Monarch's road transport including the Gold State Coach which has a maximum speed
of three miles an hour. He heads a team which includes the
Horse-box Driver of Windsor, the Rough Rider and the
intriguingly named 'Daily Ladies of London.' (Before you
ask I don't know.)

Sadly the Keeper of the Lions in the Tower, the Laundress
of the Body Linen and the Yeoman of the Sovereign's
Mouth are no longer appointed. It's nice to know the
Monarchy is gently moving into the 18th Century!

Japan – Yukigassen

For those who are uninitiated 'Yuki' means snow and
'gassen' means battle. This is a common term for a 'snowball fight' in Japanese. Cynics probably won't believe me
but, yes, 'snowball fighting' has become a professional international sport with its own rules and regulations. The
world championships are held in Hokkaido in Japan and
attract teams from Canada, Finland, Australia and the
USA, countries that host their own competitions during
the winter months. There are expected to be one hundred
teams in this year's world championship. It involves seven

players on each side with each team being provided with ninety specially formulated snowballs.

I simply cannot be bothered to explain the rest of the rules since I have an urgent desire to watch wood warp. However, I await the time when Yukigassen becomes an Olympic sport.

Court exchanges

Counsel: Immediately after you hit my client's trailer with your car what did you do?

Defendant: I woke up.

More:

The Court: The charge is the theft of frozen chickens. Are you the defendant, sir?

Defendant: No, sir, I'm the guy who stole the chickens.

And Another:

Counsel: Were you leaning up against the shut door or open door?

Witness: A shut door. How can you lean against an open door? You'd fall through the hole.

And yet Another:

The Court: All right. Any other questions?

Defendant: How can you sentence any innocent man to prison?

The Court: It is part of my job.

This is not remotely PC

District Attorney: Mr. C. you testified on your direct examination that quote: '... it takes a lot to make me angry.' Is that true?

Witness: Yes, because I don't like to get angry. I feel I can resolve problems without getting angry.

District Attorney: You figure you are basically a
peaceful person?

Witness: I try to be.

District Attorney: Your wife is named Willetta, is that
correct?

Witness: Correct

DA   On 19 December did you hit Willetta
with a two-by-four?

Witness: It was not a two-by-four. It was a
one-by-three.

An Expert Witness

District Attorney: What is the meaning of the sperm
being present?

Witness: It indicates intercourse

District Attorney: Male sperm?

Witness: That is the only kind I know.

22

LEGAL BLUNDERS

To begin this section I will share some court exchanges:

Attorney: ALL your responses MUST be oral OK? What school did you attend?

Witness: Oral.

and:

Attorney: Do you recall the time that you examined the body?

Witness: The autopsy started around 8.30 p.m.

Attorney: And Mr. Denton was dead at the time?

Witness: If not, he was dead by the time I finished.

OK, now on to serious stuff.

1820s – Old Bailey, London – England

Mr. Justice Graham was a man famous for his courtesy. He read out a list of 16 names of people to be executed. He was then informed he had overlooked John Robins. He ordered Mr. Robins be returned to the dock. He said: 'I find I have accidently omitted your name in my list of prisoners doomed to execution. It was quite accidental, I assure you, and I ask your pardon for my mistake, I am very sorry, and can only add you will be hanged with the rest.'

1978 – Manitoba – Canada

A murder trial had been proceeding for two days when a juror confessed that he was completely deaf and didn't have the faintest idea what was going on. Mr. Justice Solomon dismissed the juror from the jury. Then a second juror, a French speaker, admitted he did not understand a word of English and was surprised he was attending a murder trial. Then a third juror also said he spoke no English and, for good measure, was almost as deaf as the first juror. The judge ordered a retrial!

1990 – Carlisle – England

A judge condemned the use of £10,000 of public money over a trial which ended in the conviction of a man who had denied stealing bacon and cheese valued at £6.00.

1994 – Sunderland – England

A Sunderland man used a manhole cover to smash a shop window. He then stepped back and fell down the manhole and had to be rescued by fire crews.

1994 – Blackpool – England

David Johnson fled Kirkham Open Prison and hitched a lift. He told the driver: 'I hope you don't mind, but I am an escaped prisoner.' The driver replied: 'Not if you don't mind I am a prison officer!'

1997 – West Virginia – USA

Bill Witten swore at Judge Joseph Troisi because the learned judge had refused to reduce his bail on a charge of grand larceny. Judge Troisi immediately removed his robes, stepped down from the bench and bit Mr. Witten on the nose. The Judge was said to have a history of courtroom outbursts!

23

CURIOUS LAWS

Law is a world of wonder in which legislators pass laws and regulations which often make sense at the time they were enacted but now, sometimes, appear a little odd. Occasionally when you dig a little deeper the reason for the law becomes clear. I have said previously that if you Google 'Weird Laws' you will find endless sites listing strange laws, most of which are inaccurate. One of my favourites, even repeated by Rick Stein on one of his TV programmes, is that it is illegal to call a pig 'Napoleon' in France. It's not true.

So let me begin:

Italy – It is illegal to die

In Sellia in Italy citizens who fail to take 'preventive death measures' by getting an annual health check are fined €10 per annum. A hundred people signed up for the annual health checks following the prohibition on dying.

China – Reincarnation is illegal without the government's permission

The Chinese Government is uncomfortable with forces outside its control and has, for years, demanded the right to regulate the supernatural affairs of Tibetan Buddhist figures by determining who can and who cannot be reincarnated.

Russia – It is illegal to drive a dirty car

This law was passed in Moscow and Chelyabinsk in Russia and can garner a fine of about €30. It is suggested, cynically, this provides an excuse for the police to pull you over if they are in need of 'lunch money.'

USA – A donkey may not sleep in your bathtub after 7 p.m.

In Arizona a law was brought into force due to a public menace in 1924. A merchant used to allow his donkey to sleep in the bathtub. The town was flooded and the donkey was washed a mile down the valley. A lot of resources were spent rescuing the poor animal. The law was passed shortly after.

Italy – You must walk you dog at least three times a day

Dog owners in Turin, Italy, can be fined €500 if they don't walk their dogs at least three times a day. Germany is about to enact a law which will require dog owners to walk their dogs twice a day for at least an hour.

Samoa – It's illegal to forget your wife's birthday

The punishment is too horrible to contemplate.

Japan – Illegal to be obese

Since a law was passed in Japan in 2009, the maximum waistline for men is 85 cm (33.5 in) and 90 cm (35 in) for women. Goodness I would be in trouble.

Poland – Winnie the Pooh Banned!

In Tuszyn in Poland the local authority says Pooh Bear is inappropriate for little children on account of the fact the lower half of Pooh is unclothed.

Switzerland – You may not own only one goldfish

Switzerland has the most thorough and dedicated anti-cruelty animal laws in the world. Owning one goldfish is considered inhumane isolation. The law also applies to guinea pigs and budgerigars. An additional law mandates a training course for dog owners before they are legally entitled to own one.

Germany – Illegal to kiss on a railway platform

According to the Sunday Times of 2 February 2020 there is a regulation in Germany dating back to 1910, and still on the Statute Book, which makes it illegal to kiss on a railway platform in Germany. This is, apparently, to ensure trains are not delayed.

England – Stilton Cheese is not to be from Stilton

As the law presently stands if you produce blue veined cheese in Stilton, Cambridgeshire, you may not call it Stilton since only cheese produced at Colston Bassett, Bishop Creamery, Hartington Creamery, Long Cawson Dairy, Tuxford & Tebbutt Creamery and Webster's Dairy, which are, variously, in Leicestershire, Derbyshire and Nottinghamshire, may call the cheese they produce Stilton under the EU rule for Protected Designation of Origin status. Stilton is the only protected food name product in the whole of Europe that cannot be produced in the place after which it is named.

France – So many Mayors

There are 35,000 or so Mayors in France who are kept busy with everything from broken kerbstones to disputes about barking dogs. Some 20,000 of those Mayors preside over fewer than 500 people, a legacy of the 1789 Revolution when it was decreed there should be a Mayor wherever there was a church steeple.

USA – Indiana – What you may not do on a bus

It is illegal to ride on a bus within four hours of eating garlic. Quite right too!

USA – Nebraska – Barbers

In Waterloo, Nebraska, a barber may not eat onions between the hours of 7 a.m. and 7 p.m.

United Kingdom – Incorrigible Rogues

The Vagrancy Act 1824 was brought into force to deal with 'social ills' caused by the large number of homeless soldiers following the end of the Napoleonic Wars. Under that Act being an 'idle and disorderly person' and 'any person lodging in a tent and not giving a good account of him or herself' may be prosecuted.

24

UNUSUAL BEQUESTS IN WILLS

1788 – David Davis

Mr. Davis left the sum of five shillings to Mary Davis precisely calculated to be enough *'to enable her to get drunk for the last time at my expense.'*

1845 – John Orr and the Brides of St Cyrus

John Orr came from a wealthy family in St Cyrus, Aberdeenshire. He rose to become the Accountant General in Madras. He died in 1845 and his will provided that the annual interest arising from £1,000 was to be split between four brides, the tallest, the shortest, the youngest and the oldest. It was described as a 'welcome boon by the female sex.' The interest could, in the 19th century, equate to six months' wages for a general farm labourer. It is a tradition which persists.

1856 – Heinrich Heine

The German poet left all his assets to his wife on the one condition that she remarry *'because then there will be at least one man to regret my death.'*

1927 – Charles Vance Millar

In his will the late Mr. Millar left a prize to the mother who gave birth to the most children in the decade following his death. The race was close and frantic with $568,106 finally shared out amongst four mothers each of whom had produced nine healthy offspring. A consolation prize was awarded to one mother who had produced ten children but five had been illegitimate!

1929 – Reverend John Gwyon

The good Reverend, who sadly committed suicide, left £9,976 in his will to provide 'knickers' for the boys of his parish. (Knickers in this context refer to a sort of shorts for boys.) Sadly the gift failed because it did not fall within the definition of a 'charitable purpose.'

1955 – Juan Potomachi

Juan left 200,000 pesos to Teatro Dramatico in Buenos Aires on the sole condition his skull be preserved and used as Yorick in Hamlet.

25

RULES OF THE ROAD

1896

In January 1896 Walter Arnold was enjoying a pootle through Paddock Woods, Tunbridge Wells, Kent. He was travelling at 8 miles per hour when the speed limit was 2 miles per hour. Walter was chased for 5 miles by a policeman on a pedal cycle and was eventually caught and fined one shilling (five pence in decimal). Thus Mr. Arnold was the first person to receive a speeding ticket. At the time there were only 20 cars in Britain.

1899

In May 1899, Jacob German was driving on Lexington Avenue in Manhattan, when he became the first person in America to be pulled over for speeding. He was apprehended by a policeman on a bicycle. (You would have thought they had better things to do!)

1930

In Los Angeles in 1930 a carriage pulled by an ostrich was stopped for exceeding the 30 miles per hour speed limit.

2007

In 2007 in Geseke, Germany, Guenther Eichmann, a former engineer, was stopped for driving at 40 mph, twice the speed limit, while propelling a supercharged electric wheelchair.

2020

In January 2020 Dmitry Gromov was the first person to be prosecuted for drink-driving an electric scooter. He was fined £3,367 and banned from driving for sixteen months.

2020 – Florida – USA

A woman was driving home from Florida to North Carolina when she got a puncture. She got out and used a scissor jack to lift the car up. She had removed the damaged tyre and was moving the spare into place when the jack sank into the earth and her hands were trapped and crushed. Fortunately she had her mobile phone beside her since she had had been using the torch facility. She kicked off her shoes and after 35 minutes, using her toes, she managed to contact the emergency services. They located her using GPS. Although she had crushing injuries, remarkably there were no broken bones.

2020 – Motor insurance for golf buggies and lawnmowers

Following a decision of the European Court of Justice which has been upheld by the High Court and the Court of Appeal in the UK it seems owners of golf buggies and ride-on lawnmowers could be prosecuted if they fail to have motor insurance even though they could be driving on their own property. Despite the fact the UK is leaving the EU the decision stands unless the UK Parliament intervenes.

2020 – Nova Scotia – Canada

Lorne Grabher has a German-Austrian heritage. His family have, for twenty-seven years, driven around Nova Scotia using a personalised number which was the word 'GRAB-HER'. A single person complained and asserted the plate encouraged sexual violence against women. The Supreme Court of Nova Scotia upheld the complaint.

Mr. Grabher appealed to the Canadian Supreme Court. His basis of appeal was that his freedom of expression had been violated and thus he had been censored. The judgement of the Nova Scotia Courts was that freedom of expression did not extend to 'government owned plates' and his appeal was dismissed.

2020 – Washington State – USA

The Washington State police starting chasing a car after it hit two other vehicles in Seattle. The suspect fled, driving recklessly and at times reached speeds of 109 miles per hour. Eventually the car was stopped by the police. The driver's explanation was he was trying to teach his dog how to drive. The police confirmed there was a very sweet dog in the driver's seat but it was not steering. The driver has been charged with reckless endangerment, hit and run, driving under the influence and eluding the police. The dog has been placed under police bail.

2020 – Peterborough – England

Alex Hobbs flipped his Ford Fiesta. He then tried to persuade the police and his insurers the car had been stolen. He claimed he had been assaulted and robbed of his car. To provide some credence to his story he persuaded his friend to hit him in the face with a pan! He later pleaded guilty to wasting police time.

26

RIDICULOUS EMERGENCY CALLS

There are endless stories and, indeed, booklets devoted to the most ridiculous calls to the emergency services. The following are a few which appeal to me:

Caller: Hi, I'm having a lot of difficult breathing. My chest feels really tight and I feel faint. I might be about to pass out.

Operator: Can you tell me where you are?

Caller: I'm at the pay phone on Seward Street.

Operator: OK sir. I'm sending an ambulance to you now. Do you have emphysema or asthma?

Caller: No.

Operator: So did the shortness of breath come on suddenly? Have you any idea what caused it?

Caller: Yes. I'm being chased by the police.

A man called the police because his drug dealer had short-changed him. He claimed that he'd paid £60 for some cocaine but the amount of the drug was worth only £20.

Caller: I have lost my shoplifting ticket I was given when I was arrested last week.

Operator: .....?

A man called the police after being refused entry to a Leeds nightclub. He was being denied entry because he was too drunk, but the man ranted on until police turned up, at which point he was arrested for being drunk and disorderly.

Caller: I'm just calling to enquire about the penalties for growing marijuana. Could you tell me how much trouble you can get into for growing just one plant?

Operator: Are you in the process of committing a crime?

Caller: Err ... possibly.

Caller: I want to report my boyfriend.

Operator: What has he done?

Caller: Well for my birthday he gave me perfume.

Operator: Is that a problem? This is an emergency number.

Caller: Yes, I wanted drugs. I know he has drugs; he just won't give them to me. I can use drugs more than I can use perfume.

Operator: Are you saying your boyfriend is in possession of drugs?

Caller: Yes, of course, and I want some.

Operator: Can you give me his name and address please?

Caller: Yes, his name is ..... and he lives at .... When you get over there can you get some drugs off him for me?

Operator: Thank you for your information.

Caller: Uhh?

Caller: I want to report an intruder in my home.

Operator: Are they violent? Are they still there?

Caller: Yes, they're still here. They're probably not what you you'd call violent, no. I just want rid of them.

Operator: Do you know the intruder, sir?

Caller: Yes, it's my mother-in-law.

Operator: Your *mother-in-law?*

Caller: Yes, she's been here nearly three weeks and I want her go home. Can she be arrested for intruding?

Operator: Is this an emergency?

Caller: Of course it's an emergency. I am beginning to want to kill her.

27

TALES FROM A LAWYER'S CASEBOOK

During the time I practiced as a solicitor and, subsequently, as a Notary Public, I must have written hundreds of wills and dealt with a similar number of estates of people who had died. The following notes are of some of the matters which stand out in my memory. Before relating the various cases I would share the following observations.

It would always amuse me when a client would come to make a will and began the conversation by saying: 'If I die' and I could never resist saying, although I should not have: *'I have news for you. It's not if. It's when.'* (I am reminded of a quote from Lord Palmerston, 1784-1865 *'Die, my dear doctor? That's the last thing I shall do.'*)

Next was the paterfamilias syndrome. This was an afflic-tion which affects men rather more than women. It was the assumption that after the demise of the 'alpha male' of the family the world would not continue to turn and thus a will was unnecessary since the universe would spin off its axis and everything would be dust. As a lawyer I liked these clients since when they did surrender to father time I would make substantial fees from the mess they left behind them.

Finally, I discovered a profound truth. The only things that last are memories. Everything else is of no conse-quence. I have dealt with many cases in which memories have been tainted.

Now some cases:

Yes, you are still alive!

I have a number of clients who are entitled to pensions from Brazil, Holland, etc., who attend each year so I can confirm they are still alive. Technically a 'certificate of ex-istence.' Generally a blood pressure monitor, stethoscope and a copy of a passport suffices.

The longest estates with which I have dealt

A charming gentleman attended on me since he was anxious to finalise his late father's estate. His father, a wealthy man, had died some 76 years before in India. The lawyers who were initially instructed had died, the various companies in which the late father had invested had gone bankrupt, merged or just changed their name. But my client, who was himself quite elderly was determined to close the matter and we did succeed in the end.

A man came to see me who was originally from Jamaica. His father had died some 46 years before and he needed some forms to, at long last, finalise the estate. Later he came to see me since his mother had also died some 24 years earlier. But that was OK since in relation to the time it had taken to finalise his father's estate the period required to sort his mother's estate was, relatively speaking, supersonic.

Cases of Fraud

Notary Publics are public officials and the assumption is that public officials don't tell lies. In other words documentation to which a Notary Public attaches his or her seal has enormous weight. I have received a number of calls, specifically from Paris, Newfoundland and Dubai, in which I have been asked to confirm my seal and signature.

In every case it was a forgery. The amount of money at risk in the biggest case was £25 million.

The case of the disappearing body, Bentley car, Spanish property and jewellery

A client consulted me about her late husband, whom we will call Mr. A., who was serially unfaithful and then some. He was enjoying a sojourn on a Spanish beach with his latest paramour when he succumbed to a massive heart attack and died. An ambulance was called and the body of the late departed was removed.

Later another ambulance arrived and it was explained the body had already been removed. Anyway, to cut a long story short the people who had organised the first ambulance had arranged for various organs to be removed from his body and then deposited the remains at a local recycling site.

However, for my client that was not the end of the matter. She then discovered she did not own a property in Spain to which she thought she had title. A Bentley motor car had disappeared together with some valuable jewellery and her late husband had companies in Alderney and Mauritius and a trust in Switzerland.

Odd provisions in wills

I have received a number of requests to include odd provisions in wills. These included a man who was concerned
about the property he had purchased on the Moon, the
individual who wanted to leave his property in trust for
Jesus and the lady who wanted her wrists slashed after she
died and confirmation from two consultants she was in
fact dead.

Memorable estates

These cases reinforce my view that all you leave are memories. I had a case of a man whose wife had died far too
young. He then discovered she had a secret bank account
of which he was completely unaware which held a balance
of £250,000. He had no idea of the source of funds.

By contrast I dealt with a client who, again, had a wife
who died very young. She was, it transpired, addicted, to
online shopping. Thus after she passed away he received
many threatening letters and phone calls from credit card
companies with whom she had entered into arrangements.
More particularly she had forged his signature and taken

a second mortgage on the family home and he faced the prospect of eviction.

The very expensive pouffe and the problem of storing the late father's 'bottom'

Let us assume we have Mr. and Mrs. Jones and Mr. and Mrs. Smith. These couples had been friends for many years. Mrs. Jones sadly died leaving Mr. Jones a widower. Mr. Smith died leaving Mrs. Smith a widow. Mr. Jones and Mrs. Smith supported each other in their bereavements and eventually decided to get married.

Mr. Jones unhappily died before the nuptials. However, he had, without advising his two children, changed his will leaving Mrs. Smith an interest in his estate for the rest of her life. The children of Mr. Jones, when they discovered what their late father had done, were furious. They suggested that Mrs. Smith had an interest in their late father's house but not in the contents.

After some expensive legal debate this was agreed apart from the pouffe. The offspring of the late Mrs. Jones wanted their late mother's pouffe to which Mrs. Smith agreed but, she pointed out, she had arranged for it to be recovered and would want recompense for her expenditure. The legal costs for this literally valueless piece of furniture exceeded £1,000.

Mr. C, a widower, died leaving a son and daughter. The son had issues. In particular he was convinced he was the consequence of a liaison between his mother and a member of the royal family. When his father died he wished to retain a part of father's DNA. Foolishly I went along with his request.

I phoned the funeral director and explained the issue. The lady responded by explaining the wish was not unusual. It involved taking a 'plug' from the bottom of the deceased and then freezing it. I asked if the funeral director would be prepared to keep the 'sample' in her freezer. The answer was a firm no.

I then phoned the local hospital with a similar request and received an equally 'frosty' reply. When I broached the topic with my wife her reply was 'Anglo Saxon.'

I have no idea if the matter was resolved since the client then decided I was not fit for purpose.

28

SIGNS, QUOTES AND OTHER NONSENSE

The following are a selection of curious signs:

'OPEN SEVEN DAYS A WEEK (except Mondays)'

Sign at a New York restaurant;

'WARNING: MAY CAUSE DROWSINESS'

On a packet of sleeping tablets;

'Out for lunch, if not back by five out to dinner also'

Sign outside a photographer's studio;

'WE REPAIR WHAT YOUR HUSBAND FIXED'

Sign on repair shop door;

'THUNDERSTORMS DO NOT CALL CELL PHONES'

Sign spotted in Beijing. I have no idea.

Some quotes about old age:

'Sitting at home on a Saturday night and the phone rings and you hope it isn't for you.'

Ogden Nash (Actually he was defining middle age but you get the idea.)

'The biggest lie I tell myself is I don't need to write that down: I shall remember it.'

Anon

'There are many mysteries in old age but the greatest, surely, is this: in those adverts for walk in baths, why doesn't all the water gush out when you get in?'

Alan Coren;

'Birthdays are good for you. Statistics show that the people who have the most live longest.'

Larry Lorenzoni;

'Money cannot buy health but I'd settle for a diamond studded wheelchair.'

Dorothy Parker;

'To get back my youth I would do anything in the world, except take exercise, get up early, or be respectable.'

Oscar Wilde;

'My mother always used to say: "The older you get the better you get, unless you are a banana."'

Betty White;

'I don't need you to remind me of my age. I have a bladder to do that for me.'

Stephen Fry;

'Old age is like everything else. To make a success of it, you've got to start young'

Theodore Roosevelt

'There is no pleasure worth forgoing just for an extra three years in the geriatric ward.'

John Mortimer;

'No man knows he is young while he is young.'

G K Chesterton;

'I have discovered that alcohol taken in sufficient quantity produces all the effects of drunkenness.'

Oscar Wilde;

'There are days when one longs to be a woman.'

Gustave Flaubert. We all know that feeling;

'Start the day with a smile and get it over with.'

W. C. Fields. Exactly my philosophy.

'If you eat well and get lots of sleep and do exercise and drink lots of water you'll die anyway! So open the wine.'

Anon

I admit I am biased but I liked the following when I came across it:

From Miguel de Cervantes (1547 – 1616 Century Spanish writer) in his 'Exemplary Stories':

'... without the work of the notary truth would be hidden, shamed and ill-treated ... They pledge secrecy and loyalty and swear they will not draw up documents in exchange for money. They also swear that neither friendship nor enmity will prevent them from performing their duty with a good conscience.'

More Seriously:

'In a liberal society the law does not exist to force us into conformity, but to protect us from actual harm. It is not obvious that being offended by someone else's beliefs counts as actual harm.'

John Stuart Mill quoted by Lord Sumption, (previously a Supreme Court Judge), in the Times 9th January 2020.

Also:

'If one wishes to find truth one must first consider the opinions of those who judge differently.'

Aristotle

29

THE LAW –
QUOTATIONS
AND
DEFINITIONS

Introduction

I would like to dedicate this section to the late Dr. Julian Farrand, Q.C. a lovely man from whose advice I greatly benefitted.

I include material which I have previously dismissed for no logical or rational reasons just because... I have decided to become a little like (Sir) Billy Connolly, who has been a hero of mine since he was introduced to me by my cousin

Margaret in Kelloholm, Dumfriesshire, in which I focus on the inconsequential and ridiculous.

I am heartened by the following quote:

'It is a very sad thing that nowadays there is so little useless information.'

Oscar Wilde

My ambition and profound desire is to assist my readers to accumulate ever more useless information.

In addition let me remind my readers, once again, of Oscar Wilde's philosophy:

'I write because it gives me the greatest possible pleasure to write. If my work pleases the few, I am gratified.'

If my readers will permit me to quote Hilaire Belloc, which, according to my 'friends', is particularly apposite in my case:

'Wherever the Catholic sun doth shine, there's always laughter and good red wine. At least I've always found it to be so.'

The comment about red wine may have some resonance!

By the way, may I answer the question absolutely no one has asked: why do these booklets contain so many 'heraldic devices'. It's because I like heraldry and seek every opportunity to include it in whatever I produce.

As before the subjects included are an arbitrary choice. The only thing they have in common is that I find them interesting and/or amusing.

I shall start with law related quotes, some profound and others, I think, funny:

'No one enters suit justly, no one goes to law honestly; they rely on empty pleas, they speak lies, they conceive mischief and give birth to iniquity.'

Isaiah 59:4 (Eighth century BC approximately)

'... but if law is the master of the Government and the Government its slave then the situation of full of promise ...'

Plato (Born about 430 BC)

Hermogenes, the son of Hipponicus, said:

'Socrates, ought you not to be giving thought to what defence you are going to make?'

Socrates replied: 'Why? Do I not seem to you to have spent my whole life in preparing to defend myself? Because all my life I have been guiltless of wrong doing; and that I consider the finest preparation for a defence.'

Xenophon: Socrates' (Born about 470 BC) Defence to the Jury

'Lawyers don't know much more about law, they're just better at knowing where to find it.'

George III (1738 – 1820)

(The late King was quite right in my experience. A lawyer needs to know two things, which text book to consult, what forms you need and where to send them. That's three things actually!)

'The only obligation which I have a right to assume is to do at any time what I think right ... Law never made men a whit more just ...'

Henry David Thoreau (1817 – 1862) (Something of a hero of mine.)

'Since I'll never be famous I think I'll become a Notary and charge people for my signature.'

Anon (An in-Notary joke. You probably have to be a Notary to find it funny.)

'The right to swing my fist ends when the other man's nose begins.'

Oliver Wendell Holmes (1841-1935) (A U.S.A. Supreme Court Judge)

'These are my principles, and if you don't like them ... I have others.'

Groucho Marx (1905 -1976)

'Lex prospicit non respicit'

A legal principle which says a new rule should not be applied to a time before it was made. 'The law looks forward not backwards.'

'What's the difference between God and a lawyer?'

'God doesn't think he's a lawyer.'

Anon

'What's the difference between an accountant/actuary and a lawyer?'

'Accountants/actuaries know they are boring.'

Anon

'Lawyers are like rhinoceroses: thick skinned, short sight-ed, and always ready to charge.'

David Mellor, K.C.

A lawyer was sitting in his office when Satan appeared before him. The Devil said to the lawyer:

'I have a proposition for you. You can win every case you try for the rest of your life. Your clients will love you, your colleagues will be in awe of you and you will make a great fortune. All I want in exchange is your soul, your part-ner's soul, your children's souls, the souls of your parents, grandparents and parents-in-law and the souls of all your friends and law partners.'

The lawyer thought about this for a moment, then asked: 'So, what's the catch?'

Anon

A housewife, an accountant and a lawyer were asked:

'How much is two plus two?'

The housewife replied: 'Four.'

The accountant said: 'I think it's either three or four Let me run those figures through my spreadsheet.'

The lawyer pulled the curtains, dimmed the lights and asked: 'How much do you want it to be?'

Anon

'If a lawyer's ego was hit by lightning the lightning would have to be hospitalised.'

Kathy Lette

'... an incompetent lawyer can delay a trial for months or years. A competent lawyer can delay even longer.'

Evelle J Younger (1918 – 1989) Attorney General State of California

'To attending at your house with codicil for execution by you but you were dead – 13 shillings and 4 pence.'

A solicitor's bill sent to a (deceased) client in 1955

'If you want to be happy don't marry a lawyer.'

Matthew Parris – Times 31 March 2021

'Of my chapel choir of 17, 11 are solicitors.'

The Chaplain of Ford Open Prison speaking to Simon Brett (an author) after a talk he gave at the Prison – The Times Diary 19 October 2021

30

WEIRD CASES

I would like to pay a tribute to the late Professor Gary Slapper (1958 – 2016) who was a serious legal academic but also enjoyed the funny side of law. He was in many ways my inspiration for the booklets I have produced for the last six years. He wrote for The Times and produced three books: 'Weird Cases,' 'More Weird Cases' and 'Further Weird Cases' which I would recommend and have shamelessly mined and am about to mine again.

2003 – New Zealand

A New Zealand Telecom firm, TeamTalk, was locked in a dispute with MCS Global Digital. Both sides were concerned about the costs and delay in litigation so they decided to resolve the issue by an arm-wrestling match.

2006 – Rotorua – New Zealand

Marie Sushames returned *The Punch Library of Humour* to the public library, which she had borrowed in 1945, and said sorry it was overdue by 61 years. The fine was £3,500 but was remitted.

2008 – Melbourne – Australia

Matthew Styles was injured while working as a restaurant manager for the Red Rooster fast food outlet. The injuries were caused while Matthew repeatedly punched a customer in the face. The court decided it was a workplace injury and Mr. Styles, who was under some stress at the time, was awarded 13 weeks in lost pay.

2008 – New Zealand

Arthur Cradock phoned the emergency services claiming he was being raped by a wombat. He was sentenced to 75 hours of community services for wasting police time.

2008 – St. Paul – USA

Justin Boudin fell into an argument with a woman at a bus stop. He became aggressive and abusive. When she tried to call the police he hit her in the face. A man attempted to intervene and was similarly assaulted by a hard file which Mr. Boudin was carrying. The police had no problem tracing Mr. Boudin since his name was on the file. The file contained his homework for the anger management course he had been attending.

2009 – Alabama – USA

Sheriff Greg Bartlett from Morgan County was sent to his own jail after a judge found he had been starving prisoners in order to pocket money from their food budget. He admitted to making $212,000 over three years. One prisoner recalled having an apple during the Christmas holidays as a treat. Sheriff Bartlett was re-elected and returned to his office.

2009 – Leeds – England

Daniel Bennett had spent seven years collecting animal waste as part of his doctoral research. He claimed: 'I know more about lizard faeces than I ever thought possible.' It transpired the University of Leeds incinerated his 5 stone 7 lbs of lizard excrement. He sued in a case which went to the Court of Appeal and won.

2009 – Hamburg – Germany

Dieter Koehler, once a teacher who retired because he didn't like children, had wearied the court with over 200 court appearances. His arguments were not advanced by calling the magistracy: '... a bloody lazy bunch of layabouts.' In his last appearance he called the magistrates 'idiots' for refusing to see things his way. His abuse led to a 2-week prison sentence.

2009 – Montana – USA

Mr Erik Slye was summoned for jury service. His abrupt Anglo Saxon reply indicated he would not serve. He was contacted in writing and told he must serve unless he could demonstrate 'undue hardship.' His response on this occasion was: *'Apparently you morons didn't understand me the first time.'* He continued: *'I am not putting my family's* *wellbeing at stake to participate in this crap.'* He went on: *'I do not believe in our 'justice' system.'* Further he explained: *'Jury service is a complete waste of time.'* Placing his opinion beyond doubt Mr Slye then wrote: *'I would rather count the wrinkles on my dog's balls than sit on a jury. Get it through your thick skulls. Leave me the 'f***' alone.'*

Under threat of jail Mr Slye was summoned to court and ordered to make a humbling personal apology to all the Court Officials.

2012 – Florida – USA

Walter Weatherholt, an airboat captain, was giving a family a tour of the Everglades when an alligator attacked and bit off his hand. He was charged with 'illegally feeding an alligator.'

2012 – Australia

A female public servant was injured while having sex with a friend while on a work trip. During the sexual encounter a lamp came away from the wall above the bed and she suffered injury to her nose and mouth. In the Federal Court Judge Nicholas ruled these were injuries sustained: 'in the course of employment.'

2019 – Delhi – India

Raphael Samuel has decided to sue his parents for being born. He argues since he did not ask to be born he should be paid for the rest of his life to live. Mr. Samuel is a believer of 'anti-natalism,' a philosophy that argues life is full of misery and people should stop procreating. The consequence would be that humanity would phase out and that would be good for the planet.

Mr Samuels's Facebook page contains the following statements: *'Isn't forcing a child into this world and forcing it to have a career, kidnapping and slavery?'* and *'Your parents had you instead of a toy or a dog. You owe them nothing. You are their entertainment.'*

2021 – California – USA

A California man, Mauro Restrepo, is suing a psychic, Sophia Adams, who, he says, falsely claimed she could remove a curse put on his marriage by a witch hired by his ex-girlfriend. Mauro paid Sophia $5,100 and is seeking damages of $25,000.

Dangerous Foodstuffs

If anyone wants more information about the following cases they will have to contact me 'privately'!

A Scottish Court in 2008 confirmed a pineapple can be an 'agent of harm'.

The Supreme Court of Canada heard a case in 2009 about an arrest for the 'possession of a pie with unlawful intent.' The police stated they believed that someone in Vancouver was going to throw a pie at the Prime Minister. They arrested Cameron Ward, despite the fact he was pie-less, after the police stopped him acting on suspicion he might be 'hiding pies.' He was taken to jail and given an intimate body search. No pies were found. (It is not clear where pies could have been hidden.) He was then locked up for four hours. Cameron sued the police and won.

In 2011 Ashley Brearey from Essex, England was charged with 'assault with a dangerous sausage.' There was some discussion in court whether any injury could have been caused by a chicken drumstick. However, the matter was not resolved since the prosecution was discontinued.

In 2012 Bradley Davidson from Perth, Scotland, was accused of committing a crime with a black pudding.

31

THEY DO/DID THINGS DIFFERENTLY THERE AND THEN

Fourteenth century – Castile – Spain

King Alfonso XI of Castile (1311 – 1350) banned knights from his court whose breath smelt of garlic. He was without question ahead of his time! The smell is quite disgusting. (King Alfonso and I am correct so don't bother putting pen to paper or keyboard to e-mail!)

1568 – Netherlands

The entire population of the Netherlands was condemned to death by the Spanish Inquisition! This, I would suggest, was a bit excessive.

1613 – England

In 1613 the Archbishop of Canterbury, George Abbot (1562 -1633) was distressed after accidently shooting and killing his game-keeper. James I consoled him after telling him the Queen had killed her favourite dog in just the same manner!

1703 – England

In these days of internet fraud the case of *Regina v Jones (1703)* is interesting. A fraudster was accused of 'stealing by impersonation' with a potential fine, the equivalent today of £4,000. The judge acquitted the accused ruling: *'We are not to indict one man for making a fool of another.'* How life has changed!

1740 – Paris – France

A cow was publicly hanged for sorcery. (I am sorry what else do you need to say except how do you hang a cow?)

1819 – England

In 1819 there were 222 offences on the English Statute Book punishable by death including damaging shrubs in a public garden, larceny of property greater than a shilling, cutting a hop-bind(?) in a hops planation and breaking down the head of a fishpond so the fish might escape.

1835 – Rochdale – England

The Tory candidate for the Lancashire seat of Rochdale, a certain Mr. John Entwistle, paid 45 public houses to stay open to treat his voters. There were only 746 electors, thus, this entailed a lot of snifters per head. One elector had 36 brandies and six died before polling day from an excess of drink. John Entwistle took the seat by 43 votes.

1835 – Madagascar

Queen Ranavalona (1778 – 1861) thought it unbefitting her royal status for her subjects to dream about her so she made it illegal for them to do so.

1896 – Zanzibar

On 28 August 1896 Zanzibar and Britain were at war for between 38 and 45 minutes – no one is quite certain – making it the shortest war in recorded history! (See below for the world's longest war.)

Nineteenth/Twentieth Century – Spain

King Alfonso XIII of Spain (1886 – 1941) employed an 'Anthem Man' whose sole duty was to tell the tone-deaf King when the National Anthem was being played so he would know when to stand.

1934 – France

Samuel Tapon committed suicide in 1934 after losing the equivalent of £50,000 in an unwise speculation. At the shop at which he bought the suicide rope he haggled over the price and saved himself a few centimes. He left the equivalent of £1.5 million.

1972 – USA

Bimbo the elephant lost interest in dancing and water ski-ing after a road accident. The California Supreme Court awarded accident damages of $4,500. The name of the Judge was Turtle. (I don't why I find that funny but I do.)

1979 – Inheritance/Estate Taxes

Inheritance or estate taxes, payable on death, are very un-popular throughout the world. In the USA they have pro-duced the rallying cry 'No taxation without respiration.' On 1 July 1979 Australia abolished federal inheritance tax. There was a dip in the number of deaths in the last week of June as thrifty Aussies seemingly held on to life a little longer to ensure their heirs could inherit tax free.

1651 – 1986 The Isles of Scilly v The Netherlands (The longest running war in history)

For reasons far too complicated to explain, Admiral Maarten Tromp of the Netherlands declared war on the Isles of Scilly on 30 March 1651. In 1985 Roy Duncan, a local historian, wrote to the Dutch Embassy who replied and suggested that the Netherlands and the Islands were still, technically, at war. The Dutch Ambassador visited the Islands on 17 April 1986 to sign a peace treaty between the Isles of Scilly and the Netherlands thus bringing to an end the 'longest war in history.'

1997 – Arles – France

Jeanne Louise Calment was born on 21 February 1875 and died on 4 August 1997 making her lifespan 122 years and 164 days. She has some claim to being the oldest documented person who ever lived. She drank cheap red wine and only gave up smoking a year before her death because her eyesight was such she could not light the cigarettes.

Jeanne was married and had a daughter and grandson both of whom pre-deceased her.

Thus in 1965, with no heirs, she signed a life estate contract on her apartment with a Notary Public, André-François Raffray, selling the property in exchange for a right of occupancy and a monthly revenue of 2,500 francs (€380) until her death. Raffray died in 1995 by which time Jeanne had received more than double the apartment's value and his family had to continue making payments.

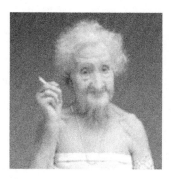

2013 – Nebraska – USA

In 1986 Donald Miller lost his job, became an alcoholic and drifted away. In 1997 on application by his wife, Robin, who wished to claim various social security benefits for herself and her children, he was declared dead. In 2005 Donald reappeared alive and well. In 2013, after making an application to the Court to apply for a driving license and social security number, he was told it was not possible to declare him alive since under Ohio law such declarations could only be made up to three years after the declared date of death. So Mr. Miller remains a legal zombie. Dead but not dead.

2015 – Italy

In 2015 Alberto Muraglia, a policeman, was filmed in his underwear clocking on. His apartment was above the police station. After clocking on Alberto would then return to his flat to get into his uniform. Alberto was sacked! In 2019, the court in Imperia has ruled it is legitimate for the officer to clock on at the start of his shift and then return home to pull on his uniform. They have *stated '... getting dressed in the morning is an integral part of the public servant's duties.' Corriere della Sera* called the decision a surprise.

2019 – France

Aurelie Boullet was a middle ranking administrator in the Aquitaine Regional Council. She claimed she was being destroyed since she had nothing to do. Her work amounted to between 12 and 15 hours a month. She once presented a report which, she was told, was in the wrong typeface. She was given a week to change it. It took her 25 seconds.

2020 – Spain

During the dreadful Coronavirus outbreak in 2020 Spain banned outdoor running and cycling. You could take a dog for a walk but not a child. (The restrictions were later eased.) Desperate Spaniards tried taking goats, chickens, pigs, canaries and even crabs out on a lead only to be fined. (I would pay good money to see a film of someone walking a crab.)

2020 – India

A 14-year-old boy in Manwai, India, seized a pigeon with a 'stamped message' on its body. The message was in Urdu, the official language of Pakistan, and also contained a Pakistani phone number. The bird was arrested by the Indian police as a 'suspected' spy. Others claimed it was simply a homing pigeon that had got lost!

2020 – North Carolina – USA

Ms. Irene Triplett died in May 2020 at the age of ninety. She was a happy and cheerful soul even in her final days so, in many ways, her death was unremarkable. However what made it extraordinary was that she was America's last surviving civil war pensioner, receiving $73.13 a month from the Government. With her death the work that began with the promise of President Lincoln in 1865 *'to care for him who shall have borne the battle, and for his widow, and his orphans'* was finally complete.

Irene's father Mose was born in 1846. He initially fought on the Confederate side and then deserted and joined the Unionists. His daughter was born when he was 83. Irene had a congenital cognitive disability that entitled her to a lifelong pension.

2020 – Paris – France

France is famous for its generous employment laws and the following may confirm that reputation. Frederic Desnard worked for Interparfums. He claimed he had so little to do that his health deteriorated. He sued his employer and has now been awarded €50,000. The court ruled he had suffered 'bore-out.' Mr. Desnard claimed, for example, if he had to buy some supplies, he would complete a few forms and then his working day was over.

It is estimated some 30% of French employees suffer from 'bore-out' because tight labour laws make it difficult to dismiss employees whose posts become redundant so, to use the French expression, they are 'cupboardised' or sidelined in the hope they will resign.

2020 – Nebraska

Nebraska got round to removing slavery as a punishment for crime only in 2020. What is extraordinary is that while 603,000 people voted for the change an astonishing 281,000 voted against.

2020 – China

A law is being introduced in China which would fine diners who fail to finish their meal in a restaurant. The law

would also ban the 'production, publication and propaga-
tion of video and audio content which promotes gluttony.'
It seems eating contests are popular in China on social
media. (There goes 'Man v Food' and 'Eddie Eats America.'
Both available on the Food Channel and are quite addic-
tive! Before you condemn try watching them.)

2020 – USA

President Trump signed an Executive Order stating that all
Federal Buildings costing more than $50 million to con-
struct must be built in the 'beautiful' classical style. This
is defined as the tradition of architecture 'derived from
forms, principles, and vocabulary of the architecture of
Greek and Roman antiquity.' Who would have thought
President Trump and King Charles would be fans of each
other!

2021 – Avignon – France

Trillade primary school in Avignon has banned parents
from throwing their children over its six-foot fence. It
seems parents who miss the 8.30 a.m. deadline have resort-
ed to heaving their offspring over the fence when they are
running late.

(Apropos of that I have been on the bridge at Avignon! It's broken!)

2021 – USA

There are 17,000 or so police departments in the USA which compares with 43 different police forces in England and Wales.

2021 – India

The Indian legal system is notorious for delays. Some estimates suggest it is clogged with 30 million pending cases. Recent examples demonstrate the point. Recently a man was cleared of murder after 36 years. Child custody cases are often decided after the child has grown up, left home and started his or her own family.

Michael Jackson performed only once in India in Mumbai in 1996. The Government promised the organisers it would repay the tax the organisers had to pay on ticket sales. After 25 years and 12 years after the singer's death the refund of £301,000 (plus interest) has finally been agreed.

2021 – France

A Bill has been presented to the Senate in France, after receiving a strong majority in the lower house, which will make it harder for visitors and new residents to take villages to court over activities that disturb them. Simply, there is increasing irritation over city dwellers who move to the country and then complain about cocks crowing, cows mooing and church bells ringing.

The Mayor of Saint André de Valborgne was so tired about complaints about animals, tractors and manure he erected a sign saying:

'Here we have church bells that peal regularly, cocks that crow very early, farmers who work to feed you. If you cannot put up with that you are not in the right place.'

2021 – Hangzhou – China

To keep track of stray dogs and prevent pet insurance fraud the city is launching an identification system by scanning canine noses. It seems a dog's nose print, like a human fingerprint, is unique. Owners are required to upload a picture of the dog's nose and then receive a digital identity card to register the dog.

2021 – Arizona – USA

The 'stupid-motorist law' is a law in the U.S. state of Arizona that states that any motorist who becomes stranded after driving around barricades to enter a flooded stretch of roadway may be charged for the cost of their rescue. The law corresponds to section 28-910 of the Arizona Revised Statutes.

2021 – France

Under a law from 1910, still in force, which was designed to stop bosses demanding non-stop labour, wine, beer and cider may still be drunk in the workplace.

2021 – Palermo – Italy

In 2013 a 32-year-old single mother attempted to leave a store with a pair of slippers, valued at €19.99, for which she had not paid. Having been caught she was distraught, returned the slippers and offered to pay for them. The shopkeeper decided to call the police. After 8 years, ten court hearings and a cost of €6,000, paid by the tax payer, a trial took place. The punishment was a one month suspended prison sentence and a €50 fine. On appeal she was acquitted because of the insignificance of the crime.

A rule was introduced in 2015 allowing the state to drop cases where the harm is insignificant but it is not much applied by Italian magistrates.

2021 – USA

A Satanic Temple is taking Boston City Council to court because it won't allow a Satanist to deliver the opening prayer at Council Meetings.

In Iowa offenders who are followers of the 'Luciferian Temple' are furious they were not allowed to keep the leftovers from their feast honouring the devil and his many good works. They could not take the remains of fried chicken, chips, popcorn and buckets of ice cream back to their cells for health and safety reasons.

2021 – Vivaro – Italy

Magistrates impounded four Italian Centauro wheeled tanks after a chicken shed was accidently bombarded during a training exercise in order to discover which one lobbed the shells. The shelling occurred during an exercise run by the Possuolo del Friuli brigade. A spokesman said it was not clear how many chickens had perished.

2021 – British Columbia – Canada

Robert Hoogland has been jailed by order of the British Columbia Supreme Court in Vancouver. His problem arises from the fact he has a fourteen-year-old daughter, the mother a lady from whom he is now separated, and was arguing against court-ordered testosterone injections for his daughter. The court declared, under the so-called Canadian 'pronoun laws,' that if either of the girl's parents referred to her 'as a girl or with female pronouns' the parent would be considered guilty of family violence.

France – Miscellaneous

I love France. Truly I do, but honesty dictates that I should record some unusual laws with which I have become acquainted.

1954 – Chateau-du-Pape

The town passed a municipal ordinance making it illegal for flying saucers to fly over or land in the town.

1959 – It is legal to marry a dead person

In 1959 a dam burst and killed 420 people. A pregnant woman who lost her fiancé was so upset President de Gaulle penned a law allowing them to be married. The authorities require proof the couple planned to marry before one of them died.

2008 – Live snails require a train ticket

Any domesticated animal under five kilos must be a paying passenger. Thus in 2008 a passenger was fined when a ticket inspector caught him carrying live snails on board a TGV.

2021 – Italy

Salvatore Scumace was hailed by the Italian media as the 'king of absenteeism' after it emerged he had earned €500,000 between 2005 and 2020 without ever working. Salvatore was 'employed' at Pugliese Ciaccio Hospital as a fire safety officer. He faces trial for extortion and fraud and has been asked to repay his wages. Another 57 employees were sent to trial for skipping work to play slot machines and go shopping.

Salvatore's absenteeism outstrips the record of a Sicilian doctor, set in 2014, who in nine years put in 15 days of work by mixing endless training courses with sick leave.

In 2015 investigators in Ran Remo caught council employees clocking on and then heading out for a day kayaking, while one was found holding down a second job as a florist.

2021 – Japan

Takashi Miyagawa has been arrested on suspicion of fraud after it was discovered he had dated 35 women telling each of them it was his birthday in order to get presents. He gave different dates to each of his potential partners after claiming he wanted a serious relationship.

2021 – Eboli – Italy

An 85-year-old man was fined twice in one day for breaking lockdown laws to meet prostitutes. He explained his friskiness was a side effect from the coronavirus vaccine. He considered the €1,000 fine for the two encounters to be money well spent!

2021 – El Puerto de Santa Maria – Spain

The 88 police officers in El Puerto de Santa Maria, according to regulations, should receive new service trousers every four years but have not received any since 2016. They claim they are tired of borrowing clothes from colleagues in other areas and have decided to go on strike. But, they have made clear, in the event of a serious incident they will respond *'... even if it is in our underwear.'*

2021 – United Kingdom

The former United Kingdom Prime Minister, Boris Johnson, recently married. I am sure we all wish him the very best. The ceremony was conducted according to the rights of the Catholic Church since Mr Johnson was revealed to be a Roman Catholic. So far so good.

However one oddity is that under the Roman Catholic Relief Act 1829 it is technically illegal for a Catholic prime minister to advise the Monarch on appointments to the Church of England. If the Prime Minister were Muslim or Hindu this would not be a problem.

2021 – France

In an effort to defeat the COVID epidemic a law was introduced to forbid supermarkets to sell 'non-essential' socks.

2021 – India

It is illegal to kiss in public.

2021 – Navarra – Spain

A Spanish court has ruled that a police officer was within his rights to arrest a waitress for serving him bad coffee! The incident occurred in 2019 when the officer stopped at a service station and asked for a large iced coffee and was unhappy about the way it had been served. An argument ensued and the officer arrested the waitress for disobedience and disturbing the peace.

2021 – Cincinnati – USA

This is a rather tangled story but let me try and explain. The drug Czar Pablo Escobar, who was killed in 1993, illegally imported hippos to his ranch in Colombia. After his death the hippos were considered too heavy to move. They have bred and now number 80.

The Columbian Government, for a variety of reasons, wish to cull or sterilise the herd and this has occasioned court cases brought by the Animal Legal Defence Fund in the US and Columbia. The US case has resulted in a decision that hippos have been recognised as people with legal rights. More precisely the hippos, in US law, have received 'interested person' status.

For information, attempts to have captive elephants declared people have repeatedly failed.

32

IT'S ALL IN
THE FAMILY –
DIVORCE AND
OTHER MATTERS

Before we look at any cases here are some quotes to focus
the mind.

*'My husband and I had our best sex during the divorce. It
was like cheating on our lawyers.'*

*'My first wife divorced me on grounds of incompatibility
and besides I think she hated me.'*

'The ideal divorce becomes relatively simple, as long as you have gone through all the groundwork of having a really miserable marriage.'

Samuel Taylor Coleridge (1772 – 1834):

'The most happy marriage I can picture or imagine to myself would be the union of a deaf man to a blind woman.'

Zsa Gabor (1917 – 2016) (who had nine husbands) once said: '... personally I know nothing about sex, I have always been married.'

OK with those thoughts in mind let us begin:

1832 – England

Joseph Thompson, a Carlisle farmer, sold his wife for twenty shillings and a Newfoundland dog. Divorce by legalised sale was still practised at that time subject to a man not selling his wife for less than one shilling!

1943 – USA

Mrs. Margaret Dayton got a divorce on the grounds of cruelty on the basis her husband forced her to eat venison every day.

In Chicago, in the same year, Mrs. Josephine Skrodenis complained that her husband, a murder story fan, took up most evenings by making her lie on the floor as a corpse while he tried to reconstruct a crime.

2002 – Glasgow – Scotland

Jean Curtis arrived home to find her husband, Ian, dressed in a blouse and rubber stockings, being intimate with a frozen chicken. She exclaimed: *'That's my Sunday lunch.'* He replied: *'It's OK. We can still eat it.'* She ejected him from the family home.

2007 – Bosnia

Sana and Adnan Klaric began divorce proceedings when they discovered their secret chat room lovers were, in fact, each other. They had poured their hearts out about the problems with their marriage under the names of Sweetie and Prince of Joy. They arranged to meet and found themselves staring at each other.

2010 – Modena – Italy

A woman, in an excess of honesty, admitted to her husband she had occasionally had a wayward thought or two about having an affair. She had never been unfaithful but she had just imagined what it would be like. The Italian Courts decided that having 'wayward' thoughts were enough to break the conjugal bond and granted the husband a divorce. Furthermore, the court ruled her dreams made her ineligible for alimony.

2011 – Chinese Couple – Kuwait

A woman was suspicions of her husband and his relationship with one of their staff. She travelled from Kuwait to China for a month's holiday. On her return she found the pet parrot repeating many phrases like: *'I love you'* and *'Be patient'* and others which were more explicit. This, in the woman's eyes, confirmed the existence of an affair and she took the parrot to the local police station and demanded her husband be arrested. In Kuwait adultery is a crime and can be severely punished. The authorities concluded they could not admit the evidence of the parrot because it could not be determined from what source the bird had picked up the expressions.

2011 – Aix-en-Provence – France

In the case of *Monique v Jean-Louis B* a wife was awarded €10,000 for injurious abstinence for her husband's lack of sexual interest. The award was made under the French Civil Code Article 1382 which says married couples agree to undertake a 'shared communal life.' The husband claimed health problems and a heavy workload which the court stated he had failed to prove.

2012 – Ras Al Khaimah

A marriage was consecrated between a 20-year-old woman and her 80-year-old husband. Within an hour the woman returned to the same court and requested the judge divorce them, reasons unknown. The husband gave his consent. This is the shortest marriage on historical record.

2016 – Moscow – Russia

Mr. and Mrs. Tsvitnenko lived in a very large three-storey house and when they divorced a decision had to be made about how it was to be divided. The judge ordered that a wall be installed dividing the house in two. Very early one morning builders arrived at Mr. Tsvitnenko's request and installed the new wall. The problem from the point of view of Mrs. Tsvitnenko was that the stairs to the upper floors were on her ex-husband's side of the house which created problems of accessing bathrooms and so on. More immediately Mrs. Tsvitnenko had a friend staying who had been sleeping in a guest bedroom on the third floor of the property. It was necessary for the Fire Brigade to be called in order that she could be released.

2016 – Saudi Arabia

A man divorced his wife because she spent the whole of the wedding night sending texts!

2016 – Azilal – Morocco

In 2014 the wife of Mr. Abragh Mohamed was involved in a serious car accident. He was advised her injuries were life threatening and it was unlikely she would survive. He travelled four hours from his village and on arrival at the hospital was informed his wife had, indeed, passed away. He received a coffin with, he was told, his wife's body inside wrapped in a shroud and he proceeded to make funeral arrangements.

Some two years later, in 2016, a woman, who turned out to be the wife of Mr. Mohamed, appeared on a Moroccan T.V. programme called 'The Disappeared' and gave Mr. Mohamed's name and address and said they had lost touch two years previously.

Mr. Mohamed does not know the identity of the woman he buried. The hospital blamed an administrative error.

2018 – London – England

An immigration officer found a novel way of ridding himself of his wife. He used his access to security databases and, during his wife's stay in Pakistan, added her name to the terrorist watch list. As a consequence his wife was unable, for three years, to return to England. His tampering went undetected until he was selected for promotion. He was dismissed.

Home Office
**Border &
Immigration Agency**

2019 – Michigan – USA

A 40-year-old man, who moved back to his parents in 2016 following a divorce, is suing his parents for $29,000 after they got rid of his porn collection. His parents admit to dumping his collection. One can only speculate on the reasons for the divorce.

2020 – Russia

I was not aware there is a condition called *'objectophilia,'* of being sexually attracted to inanimate objects. However, good luck to Rain Gordan, a young Russian woman, who has married the 'love of her life' – a metal briefcase called Gideon. It seems Gideon's hard silver-backed looks first attracted her.

Well, apparently Tracey Emin married a rock and others have married the Eiffel Tower and a 'body pillow'. (What is a 'body pillow?')

2020 – Iowa – USA

David Ostrom and his ex-wife Bridgette Ostrom were engaged in an acrimonious dispute regarding property, visitation and custody rights. Mr. Ostrom has presented a motion to the Iowa Court to demand he can confront his ex-wife or her lawyer so the matter be settled by combat, in other words by a duel. He has asked that the matter be settled 'on the field of battle where he will rend their souls from their corporeal bodies'. He claims the right to combat had been inherited from 'British' Common law and has never been explicitly banned in the United States. He quoted in support a 2016 a decision when Justice Philip Minardo of the New York Supreme Court refused to grant a request to a duel but acknowledged trials by combat had never been outlawed in the USA. The Attorney for Mrs. Ostrom, Matthew Hudson, asked the Court to order a psychological assessment of Mr. Ostrom.

2020 – Florida – USA

Sarah Boone has been arrested for the murder of her partner Jorge Torres. She had, it is claimed, zipped him into a suitcase, recorded his cries for help and then left him until he died. Her defence is that they had been drinking and they had agreed it would be funny to use the suitcase in a game of hide and seek.

2020 – France

Judge Souad Meslem discovered in 2017 that her partner of twenty years and the father of her son was having an affair. Judge Meslem accepted a posting on Réunion in the Indian Ocean. While on the island, in order to prevent her ex-partner marrying his new girlfriend, the judge faked a marriage to him. She recruited an accomplice to impersonate him and managed to produce the necessary identity papers. When Souad Meslem returned to France she announced she wanted to be known by her new married name. Her ex-partner was 'stunned' to discover he was married. The police were called and arrested the judge who is charged with 'the offence of fraudulent use of official papers by a person invested with public authority.' If convicted she faces a possible fifteen years in prison.

Colleagues of Souad Meslem, in what may be regarded as understatements, opined: *'This looks like social suicide'* and *'Her mind wasn't on the job.'*

2020 – Saskatchewan – Canada

When Philip Langan died, aged eighty, two of his seven children produced a napkin from McDonalds on which the late Mr. Langan had scrawled his children's names and the instruction 'Split my property evenly.' He had then signed his name. It is thought Mr. Langan wrote the 'will' while eating at McDonalds 'when he thought he was having a heart attack.' A Court in Saskatchewan has now recognized the napkin as Mr. Langan's last will and testament after it was challenged by one of his daughters.

The case will form part of the case law for the province which includes a will scratched on the side of a tractor by a dying farmer. On 8 June 1941 Mr. Cecil Harris was trapped under a tractor. He took out his penknife and scratched: *'In case I die in this mess I leave it all to the wife.'* The bodywork of the tractor was removed and the court decided it was a valid will.

2020 – London – England

On the rare (very rare) occasions when I advised a party getting a divorce I would always recommend they try negotiating a settlement and when they failed to try once more and to keep trying. (No one ever took my advice and wished they had when they received the lawyer's bill.) If they did not succeed the persons who would benefit most would be the lawyers. A recent case demonstrates the point.

A couple, married for 22 years and with three children spent, between them, £594,000 on lawyers leaving them with £5,000 each for themselves. Judge Robert Peel Q.C. said: *'There may be worse examples of disproportionate and ill-judged litigation but none spring readily to mind.'*

2020 – Hertfordshire – England

Venetia Murray and her brothers Dean and Dale Brunt owned a farm which they had inherited from their grandfather. In 2007 Dean died in a railway accident and it was thought he had no will with the result his £2 million share went to his mother, Marlene Brunt, who passed it to her son Dale. A lengthy legal dispute ensued which was only resolved when the solicitor's cat knocked over papers heading for the shredder which revealed Dean had made a will leaving half his interest in the farm to his sister Venetia.

2020 – Punjab – India

Amrit Kaur, an Indian Princess and the daughter of the Maharajah of Faridkot Harider Singh Brar, was distressed to find she had been disinherited when her father died in

1989. She sued the 23 people she accused of forging her late father's will and, after 28 years, the Punjab High Court has decided she is entitled to a one third share of the former royal palace in Faridkot.

2020 – Florence - Italy

A 35-year-old part time music teacher from Florence who has struggled to find work that suited him has managed to spend five years successfully arguing in Court that it remains his parent's responsibility to look after him financially. A local court concluded that the €18,000 a year he was able to earn was not enough and he could, thus, lean on his parents for maintenance. Later a Higher Court reduced his monthly cheque from €300 to €200. Now the Civil Division of the Supreme Court have concluded parents do not have an open-ended obligation to support their offspring. Parental support was not, it was decided, a lifelong insurance policy. The claimant needed to 'reduce his adolescent ambitions.' He is 35 for goodness sake.

2021 – USA

Mrs Helen Jackson died at the grand age of 101. What is remarkable is that she is the last widow of someone who fought for the Union during the American Civil War. She married James Bolin, of the 14th Missouri Cavalry, in 1936 when she was 17 and he was 93. He married for the altruistic reason that he wanted someone to inherit his pension. She did not take his name or indeed his pension. She never remarried.

2021 – Milan – Italy

Patrizia Reggiani married Maurizio Gucci, of that famous family. Maurizio divorced Patrizia for another woman with the result that, in revenge, in 1995 Patrizia paid €300,000 to a pizzeria owner to kill her husband. She was arrested three years later and imprisoned for 18 years. She later stated she had her husband killed because he *'irritated her.'* In 2017 a court ruled Patrizia could keep the €900,000 a year divorce settlement she obtained from Maurizio Gucci even though she had had him murdered. The court decided the fact she was jailed for murdering him was irrelevant – a deal is a deal and the maintenance agreement still stands.

An exchange in Court

Q   'All right, Valerie. Was there some event that finally made you decide to divorce your husband?'

A   *'Yes – He tried to kill me.'*

Q   'You felt that was the final straw?'

A   *'Right.'*

And finally:

A man seeking a divorce:

Witness: 'I just can't take it anymore. Every night she's out until midnight just going from bar to bar.'

Judge: 'What's she doing?'

Witness: 'Looking for me.'

33

SURPRISING BEQUESTS

1971 – Australia

Mrs. Myrtl Grundt, the widow of a fur dealer from Perth, left one million Australian dollars to a pair of polar bears in the local zoo.

1977 – USA – San Antonio

Mrs. Sandra West stated in her will that she wished to be buried *'... next to my husband, in my lace nightgown ... in my Ferrari, with the seat slanted comfortably.'* Her last wishes were granted subject to precautions to ensure the Ferrari was not disinterred.

1983 – England – Bristol

Tom Gribble wrote a will stipulating that on his death he be cremated and his ashes put in an egg timer so that he *'will be of some use again one day.'*

2021 – Galicia – Spain

The wife of a man named Constantino, no surname provided, sadly died in 1996. Her will, dated in 1975, specified that her husband must not remarry in order to inherit her estate. This was not uncommon provision in Spanish or indeed English wills.

The sister-in-law of Constantino, that is the sister of Constantino's late wife, brought a case against her brother-in-law who, she claimed, had started an affair with another woman in the 1980's which lasted until the other woman's death in 2016. The court decided the evidence *'proves an affectionate relationship of conjugal appearance.'* They concluded Constantino had committed a fraud against the estate and ordered him to return all the assets.

34

WHO JUDGES THE JUDGES?

King Alfred – 849 CE – 899 CE – England

King Alfred is said to have hung 44 judges in a single year for having: *'vexed the people.'* King Alfred is also known as Alfred the Great. Is that the reason?

Sixteenth/seventeenth century – England

Bishop Hugh Latimer (1487 – 1565) said, in reference to Judges: *'... they all love bribes. Bribery is a princely kind of thieving.'* To confirm the point, in 1620, Francis Bacon (1561 – 1626), the then Lord Chancellor, pleaded guilty to 21 charges of bribery and corruption.

A nineteenth century exchange in court:

Barrister to witness: *So, you were as drunk as a judge?*

Judge (interjecting):   *You mean as drunk as a lord?*

Barrister: *Yes, my lord.*

1975 – California – USA

A Judge was removed from office after demanding the Court Bailiff bring to her the police officer who had reprimanded her for a traffic offence while on her way to work. She told the Court Officer: *'Give me a gun. I'm going to shoot his balls off and give him a .38 vasectomy.'*

1992 – USA – Pennsylvania

Judge Charles Gruyer was caught on a hidden camera offering a man a lighter sentence if he allowed him to shampoo his hair. (It is said cleanliness is next to godliness!)

1993 – New York – USA

This was an ordinary dispute about someone who kept improperly parking in a handicapped zone. The case had become a little unruly and thus the Judge decided to eliminate any doubt:

Judge: Otherwise, if you want to park in a handicapped spot, I will come over and break your leg for you so you can use it legally.

Litigant: Is that a threat sir?

Judge: Next time you come to this court and make that kind of noise, you son-of-a-bitch, I will send you to jail, you got it?

Litigant: Yes.

Judge: Keep that mouth of yours shut or I will come in there myself and strangle you, you bastard. Get out of here.

2006 – Philippines – Judge Florentino Floro

The Judge asserted he could be in two places at once, was the angel of death and consulted three persons of limited growth, Armand, Luis and Angel, before making a judgement. He was eventually dismissed as mentally unfit.

2008 – Nevada – USA

Judge Elizabeth Halverson was found to:

Have fallen asleep in front of juries;

Yelled profanities;

Had improper contact with jurors; and

Had her court bailiff massage 'her feet, neck and shoulders, or some other combination of those body parts.'

She was barred from judicial office from life.

2011 – England – John Pickard

Mr. Pickard worked for the Department of Work and Pensions. His function was to assess people who were engaged in benefit fraud. In 2011 it was discovered Mr. Pickard had fraudulently claimed £18,000 in sickness and incapacity benefits. He was dismissed.

2011 – Carlisle – England

An obstreperous defendant was reprimanded for chewing gum then, when convicted, she tore out of the court screaming: *'I'm going. It's a f*****g travesty.'* This was alarming since the defendant was Judge Beatrice Bolton.

She had been convicted under the Dangerous Dogs Act 1991 after her dog bit her neighbour's son on the leg. Later Judge Bolton said, in a statement: *'I have no faith in the justice system whatsoever. I'll never set foot in a law court again.'*

2013 – Illinois – USA

Judge Cynthia Brim was acquitted of battery by successfully pleading she was insane at the time. Her attorney asserted she was 'absolutely psychotic' at the time of her arrest. Despite this she was voted in again and continued to serve for a further six years as a judge.

2019 – Wisconsin – USA

Leonard Kachinsky, a part time judge in the village of Fox Crossing, has been dismissed for making 'cat noises'. Mr. Kachinsky sought to develop a closer relationship with his female court manager who was disturbed by his advances and complained about his conduct. This included one occasion when he arrived at the courthouse, sat close to the court manager and did nothing but tap his pen and make cat noises for 45 minutes.

Retired Supreme Court Justice Simon Brown harks back in his memoirs to a previous age when he recalls a defending counsel making an over enthusiastic plea in mitigation as follows:

Counsel: *'I come therefore to urge, nay to implore, Your Lordship to show my client that self-same mead of mercy which our Lord and Saviour, Jesus Christ, extended to all mankind.'*

Judge: *'Aye, and just look where it got him.'*

2021 – Supreme Court – London

Lords Hamblen and Leggatt overturned a judgement they had previously made themselves. In doing so they quoted the words of Lord Westbury (1800 – 1873) a Lord Chancellor between 1861 and 1865: *'I can only say that I am amazed that a man of my intelligence should be guilty of giving such an opinion.'*

2021 – Leicester Crown Court – England

On 11 August 2021 Ben John was convicted of possessing information likely to be useful for preparing an act of terror, which carries a maximum sentence of 15 years in jail. Judge Timothy Spencer Q.C. concluded Ben John was a 'lonely individual with few friends.' The Judge then concluded:

'Have you read Dickens? Austen? Start with Pride and Prejudice and Dickens' A Tale of Two Cities. Shakespeare's Twelfth Night. Think about Hardy. Think about Trollope.

On 4th January I will test you and if I think you are lying to me you will suffer.'

Counsel [whispered]:　Please could you turn up the air conditioning? It's sweltering in here.

Usher:　　　　　I'm sorry, sir, I can't do that. It's controlled by the knob on the bench.

Counsel [rising]:　My lord, I understand from the usher
...

35

THAT'S NO WAY TO DIE

456 B.C.E. – Greece

Aeschylus was killed when a tortoise dropped on his head. The eagle carrying the reptile is supposed to have mistaken his bald head for a rock.

964 C.E. – Rome

Pope Leo VIII (915 – 964) had a happy end: a heart attack while committing adultery! (Can a Pope commit adultery given the fact they are supposed to be unmarried and celibate?)

1760 – Great Britain

George II (1683 – 1760) fell to his death from a toilet seat. (A fate I have only just avoided on a number of occasions usually after taking drink!)

1864 – England

Colonel Pierpoint was the man responsible for the first traffic island in Piccadilly Circus, London, to provide safe crossing for pedestrians. Stepping back to admire his work, he was knocked down and killed by a hansom cab.

1920 – Greece

King Alexander of Greece (1893 – 1920) died from blood poisoning contracted from his pet monkey.

1957 – Norway

King Haakon VII of Norway (1872 – 1957) died from complications resulting in falling into a bath. (Falling out of a bath is a risk we can all understand – well I do – but falling into a bath?)

1976 – Pakistan

A cricket umpire was beaten to death with stumps by members of the fielding side who disagreed with some of his decisions. (Since cricket is a mystery to me I have some but not much sympathy with the fielding side.)

1979 – USA

Marc Quinquadon, the world snail eating champion, collapsed and died after eating 72 snails in three minutes. (What would possess you to become the world snail eating champion?)

USA

On a lighter note Edward 'Bozo' Miller (1918 – 2008) was a Guinness World Record Holder as the 'world's greatest trencherman.' He ate 27 two-pound roast chickens at one sitting, drank 2 quarts of liquor in an hour, ate 324 raviolis in a single sitting, ate 30 lbs of elk meat, 63 Dutch apple pies in one sitting and 1000 packets of crisps.

36

LAST WORDS

Catherine de Medici (1519 – 1589)

'Ah, my God I am dead.'

Voltaire (1694 – 1778)

When asked by his father confessor if he: '... renounced the devil and all his works and pomps?' Voltaire replied: 'This is no time for making new enemies.'

Dominique Bouhours (a grammarian and priest) (1628 – 1702)

'I am about to, or, I am going to, die. Either expression is used.'

Cool.

Thomas de Mahy, Marquis de Favras (on being shown his death warrant on the scaffold in Paris, France.) (1744 - 1790)

'I see they have made three spelling mistakes.'

Even more cool.

Armand Louis de Gontaut – duc de Lauzon/duc de Biron (just before being guillotined)

'I beg a thousand pardons, my friend, but permit me to finish this last dozen of oysters.'

Super Cool.

William Pitt the Younger (Youngest ever UK Prime Minister) (1759 – 1806)

'I think I could eat one of Bellamy's meat pies.'

Lord Byron (1788 – 1824)

'Goodnight.'

Oscar Wilde (1854 – 1900)

'Either the wallpaper goes or I do.'

Anna Pavlova a Ballerina (1899 – 1931)

'Get my swan costume ready.'

Lytton Strachey (1880 – 1932)

'If this is dying I don't think much of it.'

H G Wells (1866 – 1946)

'Go away. I am all right.'

W C Fields (1880 – 1946)

'On the whole I'd rather be in Pennsylvania.'

Winston Churchill (1874 – 1965)

'Oh I am so bored with it all.'

Somerset Maugham (1874 – 1965)

'Dying is a very dull, dreary affair, and my advice to you is to have nothing whatever to do with it.'

Old Italian proverb (to put things in perspective)

'After the game the King and the pawn go into the same box.'

On a much lighter note

Bob Marley (1945 – 1981)

'Don't worry about a thing

Cause every little thing gonna be all right.'

Jimi Hendrix (1942 – 1970)

'Once you are dead you are made for life.'

And finally a couple of my favourite quotes:

'A wise man once said nothing.'

The late Captain Sir Tom Moore (Not his last words):

'The trick is to keep your mouth shut even when you're right.'

Finally, finally, please please humour me, the Latin for tomato is 'lycopersicon esculentum' meaning 'wolf peach', the Latin for rock'n'roll is: 'tumultuatio', microchip is: 'assula minuta electrica' and the Latin for burger with onions is: 'bubula hamburgensis cepulis condita'.

Who knew? Well, I suppose a Roman Centurion on Hadrian's Wall might have known. Or Julius Caesar, providing they had a local MacDonald's, for which, I am told, there is good archaeological evidence!

37

FINAL
THOUGHTS

Members of Parliament are Representatives not Delegates.
They are obliged to ignore the wishes of their constituents
if their conscience dictates.

The framers of the Constitution of the U.S.A. were concerned with the potential dangers involved in the *dictator-
ship (or tyranny) of the majority.* They put in place elaborate procedures to avoid the risks. Maybe it is something
of which the U.K. should have taken note. Fifty per cent
plus one is a majority but to ignore the views of forty nine
point nine nine percent of the population is foolhardy.

According to Jonathan Sumption, in a 2019 Reith Lecture, in one year 700 new criminal offences were created, three quarters by Government Regulation. That is in addition to the between 8000 and 12,000 – estimates vary wildly – criminal offences which already exist. Law which is not applied brings the law into disrepute and it is simply not possible to ensure thousands of criminal offences are enforced.

The following are clichés within the legal profession:

Every law will have consequences which are unexpected or directly contrary to those which are intended.

It is easier to pass a law than to repeal a law once passed.

Also By

Other books by John Kirkhope:

An Introduction to the Laws of the Duchy of Cornwall, The Scilly Isles and Devon

A Miscellany of British Traditional Customes, Ancient Laws, Eccentric Ball Games and Royal Appointments

Peculiar Laws, Ancient Customs & Curious Courts

The Duchy of Cornwall: Beyond the Law?

Co-authored with Peter Stuart Smith and shortly to be revised and republished as *The Duchy of Cornwall: Still*

Beyond the Law? following the accession of Prince Charles
to the throne

*Isles of Scilly – This Miniature Nation: A Commentary on
various matters of historical and legal interest in relation to
the Isles of Scilly*

Financial Planning for Education